Letters to Mochi

A Memoir of a Good Dog

Photo by Irma Hardjasumantri

MOCHI

Letters to Mochi

A Memoir of a Good Dog

Mary Ann Cavallaro

KDP.com 2023

ISBN-9798218150495

INTRODUCTION

You probably never knew Mochi, my gentle basset hound. She was not a movie star or a world-class athlete. Although she was beautiful, she never won a ribbon in a dog show. Probably her life was much the same as your pet's life. She loved running in the grass, lounging in the sun, and belly rubs.

Although she came to me as a frail puppy from a pet shop, by no means am I suggesting you follow my example for finding a dog. From an inquisitive and adorable puppy, she grew into a strong, happy adult animal. We gratefully shared 15 years and two weeks together.

I could just say her time had come and put her in the past–dropped from my thoughts. However, I refuse to dismiss her from my today just because she is no longer in my material world. I and I alone, determine what happens in my world of perceived awareness.

While I understand Mochi no longer wakes up in my kitchen each morning, I refuse to remove her from my world of awareness. She was my pal.

She still is my pal. Even though I am a member of this world of material reality, it does not mean I have to accept the prevailing belief that any loved one, human or animal-dog, horse, or cow, who ceases to breathe is "dead and gone" forever.

Learning from the wisdom of experience, I choose to look at life not only with flat awareness but with something deeper. The something deeper, I would like to point out does not give death its regarded power. Recognizing the limitations of my senses may be part of the problem, causing me to be unable to identify her presence in the immediate vicinity. I have chosen a broader view of the phenomenon of death and continue to believe Mochi is now part of a larger world. So if she is in a different world from the immediate world I know, why not write to her?

Positive feedback from my first book, "What My Dog Told Me About Healthy Eating," together with J. Allen Boone's "Letters to Strongheart," his beloved dog and star of silent feature films, inspired me to write to Mochi.

If you continue to read the following chapters, you will see the letters I wrote to Mochi, accepted by society as a dead dog. Since writing to a dead dog is not common practice, I thought you might appreciate some explanations. The following pages give a view of the life we shared and the love that goes beyond. While the letters each stand on their own, remember they are meant for and written to Mochi, which puts you in the position of reading over her shoulder, in a way. I hope it will be a rewarding experience.

Mochi did not arrive in my household, already bonded with me. Trust and love developed over time and with much effort on both our parts. You may have heard of the expression "Good Dogs–Great Owners" from Brian Kilcommons' book, likewise entitled. In all honesty, I would never call myself a "great owner," but I would describe Mochi as a "great dog." Animals want to get along with humans, while humans wish to share responsibility for creating a cooperative relationship based on respect and fairness. Animals need to become themselves, just as we need to find out who we are.

Mochi's love and sweet-tempered disposition during our years together guided me through my relationships and encouraged a deeper kinship with animals as well as humans. This relationship became an important part of my life, perhaps just as the connection between you and your pet has become a part of your life.

If you continue to read on, maybe my letters to Mochi will comfort you and deepen your bond with your good friend, whether she is at your side or in your heart.

To peace and permanence, in the loving memory of my beloved, Mochi, and all those who crossed her path.

Mochi is a Japanese rice cake many times used as a dessert, the happy part of a meal.

Contents

Chapter 1

BREATH

Princeton, New Jersey
Midday, July

To Mochi
Backyard in the sky
Dear Sweetheart,

Ever since that Fourth of July when you gave me my unwanted independence and took yours by going to another world, I still have so much I want to tell you. Some things are routine but treasured, while others are deeply personal between us and I feel uncomfortable discussing with most human beings. So I am writing to you. Our life together was always a conversation.

You know as well as I do that even though I cannot pet your furry head or feel your long, solid body, our friendship not only still exists but will exist into eternity. Mentally, I am always within your reach as you are within mine. Of course, I miss being able to greet you when I come down into the kitchen each morning. Our kitchen misses you. Our whole little house misses you. Our backyard misses you. The tree where you drank water that collected in its trunk misses you. The neighborhood misses seeing you on our morning walks. But I know you are OK where you are, running and happy every day in my time or eternally in your time. You are as much a part of the eternal plan as I am. Mochi, you are as eternal as your virtues.

Yes, the weekend vet in the emergency room pronounced you dead that day while my friends expressed sadness but no surprise. "Dogs die," they said. Or as our regular vet said the next day when he called me, trying to help, "You don't see many fifteen-year-old basset hounds walking around." As if to say it was your time to leave, and I should be grateful for having had you for so long. Or as a neighbor put it in another attempt to help me feel better; "Get a new dog," as if you were a commodity.

I'd like to tell them, "My Mochi, dead? What do you think she was made of? Pounds of bones and muscles with some energy inside that ceased to sparkle. If you think that, you are wrong!"

You are looking at her through your eyes that see only the material world or maybe eyes that are not open. What you were not seeing were Mochi's qualities. In some fairness, since I was closer to her, it is easier for me to see those qualities of hers that were so precious and admirable: Sweetness, goofiness, sincerity, honesty, goodness, gratefulness, loyalty, love, affection, devotion, inquisitiveness and the list goes on!

Qualities, not material matter! And the highest qualities at that! Qualities that made me love her. Mochi is as everlasting as her virtues! Her qualities are in my heart. They are a part of me, just as they were a part of her. They are like breath and cannot be buried in the ground any more than you can bury the air you breathe. Her attributes cannot be burned into ashes and sprinkled over the earth or stored in a box. Mochi's qualities are eternal."

Right now, you seem to be beyond my human sight, the call of my voice or the grasp of my arms. As much as I want to, I do not know how to play our favorite backyard running game, with you running around the yard while I clap my hands. But that is my problem, a human problem. We, humans, have a tendency to perceive life with distorted vision as to what is happening to the people and material objects around us.

We focus our thought processes along these distorted lines often inward, backward, or downward rather than outward, forward, and upward. We focus on material objects of all kinds-- the almighty dollar, a new house, an SUV, the big vacation to a far-off country, and the list goes on and on. We are taught at birth to constantly achieve and consume till we die. No wonder we sometimes feel as if we are living restless or useless lives.

Mochi, if you were a human they would have conceded, like the vet, that you were old, had lived out your life and now were in your eternal resting place. But being only a dog, you are just flatly dead. There is at least one person who does not believe this, me!

True, it's just one vote that you are not out of existence, but every vote counts! You are with me every day, though not as a part of my material world, which is mostly useless anyway, but alive!

Let others believe you are dead if that is what they want to think. They are entitled to their thoughts, but I know otherwise. I know the magnitude of the real you!

I'll be seeing you....

Photo by Robert Thorpe

Chapter 2

MORNING DARKNESS

Grand Canyon, Arizona
Morning, July

To Mochi
Backyard in the Sky
Dear Sweetheart,
    I am up high standing on the top of a
mountain surrounded by darkness, but feeling safe.

Like you, I am afraid of heights. There is early morning darkness on top of a mountain at Mather Point on the South Rim of the Grand Canyon. I wanted to see the sunrise. I needed to be in these sky lands of spiritual free-thinking to tell you again that you *are* my beloved dog, not a dog of the past. So I boarded the first run of the morning park shuttle, sat in one of the few remaining seats as we winded up the mountain, disembarked in the blackness and here I am.

Looking up, the heavens above me feel so close, so close to you. The darkness around me seems to be on my standing level with nothing beyond or below. My feet are firmly planted on a huge rock.

Actually, I am not physically alone on the mountain. At least 100 people are on the mountain in the Grand Canyon, this July morning, standing on the surrounding ridge to watch the sunrise. Most of them are hidden in the morning darkness with only the closest visitors visible. On the same rock on which I stand, a man is standing a few steps higher up, about nine yards away wrapped in a white blanket that looks like it came from his hotel room. But spiritually I am alone.

Alone with thoughts of you and this phenomenon called death that is supposed to have removed you from the earth and taken you away from me forever.

Death has always frightened me because it is a journey into the great unknown. Even if life here is a challenge, the hardships of a cancer diagnosis, the loss of a lover, the loss of a job, or a dying father always seem better than the great unknown.

Death is sorrowful because it takes people and animals away from humans and other animals that are still here on earth. If we are born, we are sure to die.

In the immortal words of Mark Twain, "The only two certainties in life are death and taxes." Few have questioned it or tried to explore it. At funerals, people sing hymns about "fighting the good fight." We want to stay alive as long as we can and keep others with us as long as possible even if they are in a non-active state.

What happens after death is the issue that troubles, baffles, and causes great controversy. This has gone on for centuries. Some believe that through death we reach a glorious place, our reward for living a compassionate life. Others believe we are assigned a miserable place as punishment for a heartless life. The process itself can be another belief system. And still, others believe death is the end and there is nothing after, whether it happens to a human or a hound like you, Mochi.

I remember the time I looked at you as an old dog and wondered if you felt the same as me about aging, resigned. We were sitting in the kitchen and I looked into your brown eyes. The fur on your face was white. Do animals like you understand they are aging and life with their human family will end? I think they do.

But today there is a movement to look closer at death. In healthcare, there is a term for it, hospice. The terminally ill are no longer shunned but respected and accompanied on their journey to the next world. Maybe we are looking closer at death because people are living longer and are discussing their impending future. Huddled in the dark, thinking these dark thoughts I continued to stare out at the distant mountains. The air like my thoughts felt heavy.

Then I saw it in the dark distant mountainous crater: a fire was rising, a reddish blackish powerful light with traces of white; one of

the brightest lights I have ever seen! I felt a life
force, your life force rising like the sun within my
being! I felt the surge of our love! The fire and
light spread out from the hole; dawn was breaking.

Could the Divine Designer of such an
extraordinary scene also create something as
diabolical as death? The thought seemed ludicrous.

All the while the morning darkness receded.
Gradually, I could see that the rock I was standing
on was jutting out from the mountain surrounded
by an endless drop. I was standing on a ledge!
Being fearful of heights, I should have been
frightened, but I wasn't. I was in awe at the beauty
of the morning on the mountain while you were
with me.

Death is nothing more than the morning
darkness that surrounds the mountains that exist,
though invisible till the dawn breaks. The morning
darkness does not change what is there but is just a
temporary barrier. It is nothing to be afraid of since
the mountains, solid as ever are there but just can't
be seen.

I must admit that the darkness of death does
surround us separating us from each other until the
break of dawn. But the darkness never penetrates

the part of my heart where my love and thoughts of you have lived ever since the first day I met you. Nothing in the morning darkness can ever touch the bond between us. That is why I know, My Sweetheart, that all is good with you and between us.

I'll be seeing you...

Chapter 3

EARTH TONES

Grand Canyon, Arizona
Morning, July

To Mochi
Backyard in the Sky
Dear Sweetheart,

After spending two more wonderful days in the Grand Canyon, riding the internal transport bus, hopping off at its frequent stops to explore on foot the clay-colored trails among the desert-like shrubs, I let my feet take me in a different direction.

Leaving the Canyon, I travel along an eastern route to Colorado. But before I say *adios* to the terracotta mountains, I want to talk again about this condition called death. I'll say it for the two of us as we are thought to be on different sides of it. The accepted belief has you counted as a dead dog and me as a live human. Let's get into it before I get ready to board the transport van to Flagstaff.

Death is humankind's most mysterious and feared event. It happens to everyone. It is accepted as inevitable by everyone that if we are living, we will eventually die. But why must we die? How did something as horrible as death get into practice?

It's a frequent question we never stop asking. "Why do people we love have to leave us never to see them again?" Many times, they leave us in the most painful of circumstances. What happens to them during death? Where do they go after they die, if they go anywhere? Is there anything beyond death? Do they go to a 'better place' after they die? What is that 'better place' like and who goes there? Is it only for the sanctified or esteemed ones? Where is that 'better place'? And what about the animals-- birds, fish, insects, the four-legged and so on?

Where do they go after they die, if they go anywhere? Will we ever see our beloved pets again? What about the millions of animals slaughtered each day that had no one to love them? Where do they go-if they go anywhere? Do we humans have a better chance than other forms of life of attaining this continuation after whatever follows our present time on this earth?

These are very heavy questions and when they come to mind in a fast series, I have to stop and think a little. "Think" is the keyword here. I can choose what I wish to think and consequently believe it. I can sift through my thoughts. If events are happening in the world around me and I know about them they are inside the awareness of my mind not outside of it. If I know of the events they must be inside my world. The universe is therefore not external but internal. The universe is part of me.

But what about people, animals and objects that the senses report as separate or detached from me? Are these too, psychic notions in my world of awareness? If my argument moved in that direction it bumped up against an object, my physical body? Do I live inside my physical body or is this too part of the notion of my world of awareness?

The general consensus believes we live inside our frames and we possess an equilibrium system that allows us to move our frames about. Information from the "outside world" is obtained through our five senses, sight, hearing, taste, touch and smell. This idea never seemed to go far enough for me. If this is the case, we are prisoners of our bodies.

I don't want to sound morbid, but whenever I visit my parents' graves in the church cemetery, I picture their bodies inside their boxes and wonder where their essence is. It is not underground. They must be somewhere else. Maybe their bodies are there decomposing but surely, they must be somewhere else. If it sounds confusing it is.

Still sifting, let me approach the issue from the other side. What if I lived outside my physical body? My body frame and all its enhancements like, skin, bones, and fluids are mine though not me. My body is mine but not me. I'm more than my body. I have my own identity or inner self. Levels of consciousness make up my inner self. This highest level of consciousness I will take with me no matter where I eventually go.

This identity, inner self, levels of consciousness or awareness are me! This thought gives me tremendous comfort. It actually takes away some fear.

The idea also seems consistent with the people who have out of body experiences. They may see their body left behind but have an opportunity to return to it.

What about the moment of death? I was not aware of the moment of birth, not even the whole process of birth. Of course, I eventually heard about the event from my mother later. So, taking this approach to death, it is unlikely that I will die, according to my reasoning, because if death brings the end of mental awareness, then I cannot be aware that my physical body is experiencing death.

So, death must happen to that other guy, my physical body, not my awareness, my identity. This is quite a responsibility. I have to stay alive to continue thinking. As long as I can keep thinking, there is no death to that other guy.

I am in my universe and choose my thoughts, experiencing only my universe. As a creative thinker, the mystery of death is up to me. Going further, I identify only those people, animals or physical objects who are in my universe. If they made it into my universe, it seems only right that I am responsible for them, and for my thoughts about them: quite a situation, quite an obligation! So, in other words, if someone dies, the process happens in my universe. I have to agree that he or she is dying since I am in charge of the thoughts in my world. I declare her dead, departed from my universe. I break the links between us.

Mentally I dig the grave and shovel the dirt on top of her box or urn. I decide that she is gone from my world forever. This happens within my consciousness, with my agreement and with my assistance. How morbid! My world is transformed into a graveyard of ghastly concepts about a world that was made by the Creator who loves us and wants to share His love. Something is wrong with this picture.

And now about our picture. You were not in my world until I let you in. Actually, you were brought in by someone who loved me. You gave me tremendous companionship with daily chuckles. You helped me discover new meanings of love, loyalty and God's universe. And now because my human body with its supposedly sophisticated senses cannot identify your material body, society would have me put your urn in a bottom drawer or basement or some other place to be forgotten. What a way to treat a friend. What a way to treat a beloved friend like you!

Dead? You? Not in my universe. I would never allow such a thing and I believe you would do the same for me. You dead? Outrageous! We both know too much about love, don't we?

I'll be seeing you....

Chapter 4

HONEY

Grand Canyon, Arizona
Morning, July

To Mochi
Backyard in the Sky
Dear Sweetheart,

More than ready to leave the Grand Canyon, I boarded the transport van. There was barely room to sit. Just like the Canyon, the van was crowded with people. An older couple traveling with their service dog took up two seats while their Irish Setter took up a substantial amount of floor space. A young couple and a small child overloaded another two seats.

The child's mother cuddled the little one in her lap while the father sat beside her. This minivan would take me to a connection in Flagstaff, Arizona to eventually reach Grand Junction, Colorado. Needing more time to chill, I chose to go to a place where I could meet, and hopefully commune with more animals. Colorado and wild horse country seemed to be the right place.

A couple of days after you changed worlds, I visited with a horse named Honey. Her person, Danielle, was the young woman who stayed with you when I traveled during the last year you lived in our house. When she and I met, we instantly connected. We each sensed our love of animals and there were never any reservations about her being your live-in dog sitter. I am glad you got to meet Danielle, but I wish you could have also met Honey. Unfortunately, Honey could not leave the farm where she was boarded, and dogs were not allowed in the barn. Danielle always urged me to come down to her barn and meet Honey, but I never felt a need to take her up on her offer until a few weeks after the Fourth of July.

Unlike her sweet name, Honey is an unruly horse with a mind of her own -- and what a mind! The afternoon Danielle and I went out to the field, seeing us at a distance, head up, she ran in our direction, slowing down to a walk as she came near us. Even at a distance, I could feel the powerful energy of her lean body moving toward us, becoming stronger and stronger as she came close to us.

After greeting Danielle, tilting her head, her alert eyes looked at me with some sort of understanding. Petting her was comforting to me and perhaps also to her since she nestled her nose in the center of my chest. Feeling her breath on my face, I breathed right back to her from my nose to her nose. This old South American Indian custom of connecting seemed to be working with Honey that day creating a bond.

While we walked with Honey around the paddock, Danielle spoke about how she had gone from horse trainer to horse trainer in search of someone to help her manage her mare.

When Danielle bought Honey, she did not know that she was a horse accustomed to jumping, a high-risk practice. Nor was she aware that Honey had cuts in her mouth that indicated she had been abused with her bridal and mouth bit.

Danielle pursued private lessons to gain cooperation from her new horse. She told me she spent the majority of private lesson time punishing Honey for her behavior. "Punishing" by walking her backwards when she could not complete the task by going forward. Eventually, Danielle found a gentler trainer who was able to offer some help. After she had gained experience, she decided to use a softer approach and manage Honey herself. She also found she could communicate with the big brown horse directly, talking to her as if she were talking to a person just the way I always talk to you.

When you first came to live with me, as a puppy, I also struggled to communicate with you. Even though constantly caring for you, taking you out in the back yard every three to four hours day and night, walking daily around the neighborhood, two-way communication was almost nonexistent. Since I assumed that the human, me, should be giving directions to the animal, you, it took me a while to learn that there was a different way to do things. It did not happen when you were a puppy but rather when both of us were a little older. After attending two dog "behavior training" classes, flunking one, consulting with veterinarians, reading volumes of books and countless magazine articles, watching endless videos and comparing notes with numerous dog owners until an animal communicator in the local pet store suggested I talk to you, just as I talk to people.

Such a simple idea! With a quiet mind, your answers would come through to me. Why hadn't I thought of it? That is how our conversation started and continues today. There are many opinions about dogs and animals and there are facts about dogs and animals. Experience taught me that animals have the facts and humans have the opinions. It seemed only natural to go directly to the source. At about that time, I also realized that I was the less intelligent of the two of us. Just like Danielle and Honey- it is between me and you.

In addition to talking with you, my own pet, many times your furry relatives teach me more about other animals or people than humans can ever teach me, which is why I chose to go to wild horse country.

I'll be seeing you...

Chapter 5

HONEY STANDING TALL

Grand Canyon, Arizona
Morning, July

To Mochi
Backyard in the Sky
Dear Sweetheart,

One more memory of Honey, the powerful communicator came to mind, as I boarded the transport van to Flagstaff where I picked up my connection to the airport.

"Can you come out to the barn and help me with, Honey?" Danielle texted. Never before have I heard her ask for help with her big brown horse. Something must be wrong. I drove over to the barn and found Honey with a swollen ankle and hoof.

During the night while grazing outside in the field, her shoe came off and she stepped on one of the nails that holds it in place. Although the barn workers where Honey is boarded immediately notified Danielle in the morning, the hoof and ankle were already infected.

A Veterinarian arrived, dressed the wound and put Honey on antibiotics. The dressing needed changing every day. Since Honey is a very high-strung horse, the job required two people; one to hold her while the other changed the dressing. For the first two days, Danielle, who usually visits Honey alone, obtained help from her mother and boyfriend.

Today neither was available. I am not a very strong person while Honey is an extremely large and powerful horse. Many times, when I arrived at the barn, she would put her head in my coat pocket looking for carrots, almost knocking me over with the swing of her neck. But today I was determined to be the designated helper.

Approaching slowly, I held Honey's halter and fed her carrots while Danielle changed the dressing on her right front hoof. It was serious business. I knew, as I believed Honey knew, something was seriously wrong. A horse that can't walk will not be alive for long.

I am always a little afraid of horses, but my fears seemed to be stilled as Honey was quiet with me. She sensed my determination to help her. Calm, she was neither stomping nor snorting as was her usual behavior. With my head close to hers, we looked into each other's eyes. We formed a bond just like the bond I always felt with you, especially when you were sick.

Although Honey was the one who was 'sick,' I needed her for my ailment. When you and I lived with each other, we needed each other even though we were both healthy for the majority of our years together. When either of us was sick the need was greater.

Would the swelling subside? Would Honey be able to continue to stand on her swollen leg? I wondered as I drove home that day. The possibilities were frightening to think about.

Danielle needed my assistance again, the next day. This time I returned to the barn with hesitancy, fearing the worst: but something had changed. Amazed I found Honey standing, bearing weight on all four legs and acting more like her impatient self, but we still had our bond.

Taking my position, holding her harness with our heads close together looking into each other's eyes, we both knew we would be making a complete recovery.

Even with her injury, Honey still knew how to console.

I'll be seeing you…

Chapter 6

CATS

"Dogs and cats play and are at peace with each other, and they do not feel lonely for you. They miss you, but with the special wisdom that animals have, they trust that this condition will get better."

Wallace Sife

Flagstaff, Arizona
Noontime, July

To Mochi
Backyard in the Sky
Dear Sweetheart,

It was a relief to stand and step off the transport van in Flagstaff. In the winter Flagstaff is a ski resort receiving blankets of snow, but on this July day, it was hot with an impending rain storm. Like many of the old Western Towns, it is nestled in a mountain beneath wide-open blue skies and surrounded by distant mountains. Coming into view from a higher distance above the parking lot where we were dropped off, were a few blocks of beautiful old concrete buildings and a couple of church steeples.

While waiting for my next connection to the airport, I wandered down the narrow street into Biff's Bagels, a nearby bagel shop. Entering the small café, a strange feeling came over me: sadness. Pictures of dogs covered the walls. As I stared at the pictures, the dates under each dog's picture became visible. These animals were somewhere in another world. A friendly man in his 50s came up to the counter to wait on me; the owner. He confirmed my thoughts, as I sipped my coffee and chatted with him.

"Just before we opened the café, my dog died. That's his picture over there," the owner said, pointing to a picture of a large furry dog mix with bright eyes, "Biff." Hanging up his picture gives me some comfort. When customers see it, they bring in their own photos. The pictures just keep coming."

"My dog just passed," I said.

"I'm sorry. Did you create any memorials?"

"A memorial stone with a US flag by its side is in the back yard-she died on the 4th of July. A canvas picture is in my den and a framed picture sits on my dresser, next to her ashes."

I see, his eyes said.

"When I get home, I'd like to send you a picture of my dog for your wall."

"You are welcome to do that. Just keep it small because pictures are coming in all the time."

As I sipped the last drops of my coffee the sky grew darker with impending rain. There was no hurry; the transport van wasn't due to arrive for an hour at the Flagstaff Tourist Center place of pick up. I decided to risk the rain, thinking that it might be possible to board the earlier transport listed on the online schedule. I was impatient, to leave the heavy feeling of the café. Although the café was normally an upbeat place, my mood and our conversation made me restless. Rolling my one green suitcase toward the front door, I turned and took one last look at the fury faces on the walls of Biff's Bagels. "Mochi, your picture will look good there," I whispered.

The sidewalk was very narrow and the wheels of my suitcase bumped along the pavement. I felt the first raindrops. I walked a little faster, as the drops quickly felt stronger. There was still a distance to go. Two more blocks and then I had to cross a wide street lined with railroad tracks in order to reach the Information Center.

The rain was now coming down in torrents. My non-leather waterproof hiking shoes were holding up but my rain slicker seemed to lose its waterproof abilities. Walking turned into running. Up until this time, I remained calm, but panic set in as I watched the water flooding down the street with the narrow sidewalk creating a sort of pipe effect that caused the water to barrel forward. My suitcase felt bigger and heavier.

Would my clothes get wet? It was supposed to be waterproof, but so was my slicker and I was soaked. As I came to the end of the last block, just before the railroad tracks, I noticed a corner store, a pizza place with water splashing up its front door. It had a large window with a ledge where I had a fleeting glimpse of two cats perched snuggling together dry. Whizzing by, they looked at me. Perhaps they were wondering why this woman was running with a suitcase in tow in a rainstorm rather than seeking shelter in one of the many buildings or places on the street.

The railroad tracks were buried under water. I lifted my suitcase as high as I could as I ran across the tracks. Drenched, my waterproof hiking shoes were totally underwater.

Swinging open the door of the information center, I burst into the waiting room dripping and wild. Two women behind the counter calmly looked up at me, and then lowered their heads returning to whatever they were doing.

"Is there a bathroom available?" I asked. Since we were the only people in the room, hopefully, they would figure out I was addressing them. Both women looked up again. "Down the hall on the left," one responded, pointing to a hallway behind me.

My thoughts as I turned toward the hallway were on my soaking wet suitcase and probably clothes—for nothing. Once inside the restroom, to my great relief, I found that my clothes inside the suitcase were dry. My cheap synthetic bag had done its job. However, my clothes under my expensive rain slicker were very wet.

Changing into something dry brought a feeling of confidence. Returning to the waiting room, I sat on one of the benches. The two women behind the counter continued to be deep into their project until interrupted when a large brown tabby-colored cat jumped lightly onto the counter from somewhere underneath it. For a minute I thought one of the cats out in the storm had followed me. Looking more closely, I noticed that this cat was dry!

As it walked down the counter, its long tail brushed the shoulder of one of the women. Without lifting her head, she immediately raised her arm to stroke her large round soft body. In return, the cat snuggled her. With all due respect to cats, their intelligence has never impressed me. Entitlement and raw instinct better describe them. The ladies behind the counter caught my stare and seemed to have read my mind.

"Cats are curious as well as loving," one of them said. "Our Gracie was coming out to see our newest visitor who braved the rain."

The chaotic workings of my mind seemed to still ramble over the cats reacting to me. However, if the cats thought that fighting something inevitable, but eventually passing was a waste of time and effort, then this trio made it a unanimous opinion.

I settled back in what looked like a church pew in the Visitors Center, closed my eyes to clear my thinking, and heard a little swish next to me.

Opening my eyes, I noticed Gracie seated at my side looking up at me with a little twinkle in her eyes.

I'll be seeing you...

Chapter 7

WILD HORSE RANGE
When you wake in the morning hush;
I am the swift uplifting rush
of quiet birds in circling flight.
I am the soft starlight at night.
Do not stand at my grave and weep
I am not there
I do not sleep.

An Indian Prayer

Little Book Cliffs
Grand Junction, Colorado
Early Morning, August

To Mochi
Backyard in the Sky
Dear Sweetheart,

Since my last letter, I have safely arrived in Grand
Junction, Colorado and am staying with my friend,
Flo. Surely you remember Flo, the lady who
visited you sometimes when I was absent for a day
or when Danielle was house sitting and away at
work. It was Flo who made the wild mustang
expedition possible.

Twenty minutes from Flo's house, about eight miles northeast of Grand Junction there is an area owned by the Federal Bureau of Land Management where wild horses roam. Only four-wheel drive vehicles are permitted to operate in this rugged area of cliffs and steep dirt roads. We only had my friend's Honda CRV parked in her driveway ready for use.

Flo's friend Peter is a retired Navy nurse with plenty of time on his hands. Single without children or pets he had few hobbies and a handful of friends, namely Flo whom he adored. Peter owned a four-wheel-drive truck and was only too happy to drive Flo and me to Little Book Cliffs.

The temperature climbed to 100 degrees at 7:00 am on that Saturday morning. Peter pulled into Flo's driveway with his four-wheeler. Flo climbed into a seat in the back while I jumped into the front seat next to Peter. There was little traffic on the road as we made our way to Little Book Cliffs. It's estimated that 124 horses roam this 36,000-acre range.

There were two routes. One was closer which took us to a ridge where we could look down. The other needed the four-wheel-drive vehicle to take us up the mountain. As you know, driving up a mountain is not one of my strong points but my excitement was high as we ascended the back of Mount Garfield by way of Coal Canyon Road.

Fortunately, Peter focused on driving and said nothing about my gripping the seat and leaning close to him almost sitting in his lap while peering out over my passenger side window. Each time the four-wheeler lurched, I was sure we would tumble over the side and fall down into an eternal opening!

Flo on the other hand sat back, relaxed and enjoyed the view. Not only were there no horses to be seen, there were no signs of life on the mountain during our short but seemingly forever crawl to the top. We passed one or two metal tanks that looked abandoned. Peter, who drove as if he was on his daily commute to work, pointed out they were not abandoned but used as water tanks.

I felt relieved when Peter easily pulled off the dirt road into what looked like a small parking area. Stepping out of the vehicle, Peter and Flo began chattering between themselves so I drifted out on my own among the low-growing shrubs.

Disappointment mounted, as I saw a tiny

bird perched on one of the shrubs. Silent she just fluttered her little wings and took off. It was still. The air felt thin while the big blue sky felt so close. No horses were anywhere to be seen. With the hard dry ground, they would not have left a trail even if they had been there.

In sync, all three of us regrouped and got back into the truck. Peter drove down to the ridge. Even driving the easier route to the ridge unnerved me. Mentally I tried through the universe, to communicate with any horses in the area, sending love. Before I could think of what I was saying I asked Peter if he had any firearms in the truck. Wild animals many times can sense the violent possessions of humans. If my question sounded strange to him, he did not let on.

Again, Peter pulled off the treacherous road into another small parking area where only from this place, a dirt trail led to the cliffs. Hope returned.

However, neither horses were to be seen or heard, nor any tiny birds. Visible were only these strange shrub-like bushes on the narrow path that led to a large old gate.

Walking up this path we strolled through the

gate onto a dirt trail that wound around the mountain. On one side the mountain bordered the trail while on the other there was a sheer drop into the hard dry barren canyon below. What a wonderful view we would have if horses walked through this canyon. Eagerly looking upward and outward above the canyon, I had hoped to see some movement, but there was none.

Again, in silence, we took a few steps toward the first bend of the narrow mountain trail. A few steps were all we wanted to take. Unless we were interested in hiking, which we were not, it made no sense to go any further in this barren place without any sign of horses or animals. I must confess, I again breathed a little sigh of relief as we turned and walked back out the gate and down the dirt path to the parking lot. The drop on the side of the narrow mountain trail made me cringe.

I walked on the outside with Peter next to me and Flo beside him. This time they compared the brand of their water bottles.

Suddenly I felt a nudge on my right thigh. Looking down I saw a black lab whizzing by me with his tail wagging. He went over to Flo, continued downhill and then turned and ran uphill toward the ridge. How sad, I thought, a dog lost on this mountain. I looked for his person never expecting to see one in this remote place. The dog disappeared for a minute and then I saw her, a woman walking a basset hound on a leash.

Surprised and overjoyed, I ran to the lady and asked if I could pet her dog, a beautiful small basset your size, but with a lighter brown coat than yours. Her person, a friendly middle-aged woman, said her dog's name was Cleo and she was on a leash because many times she did not want to return when it was time. I told her person about you and how you never listened and refused to go home when on a walk in the neighborhood.

Cleo let me pet her. Before we parted I stood back, looked at her and stroked her left ear, just as I had done to you a hundred times including the last time, I saw you. Cleo's friend said she had seen horses about three weeks before after a heavy rain when the creek had running water. Since the heat returned and the creek had dried up, she believed the horses had gone back up into the mountain where it was cooler. She told us she frequently walked her two dogs there on the ridge and often saw the wild mustangs. It was good for Flo and Peter to realize this. They had not been taken on a wild goose chase after all.

Not seeing any wild mustangs was no longer disappointing since I had seen a basset hound like you. Cleo was a reminder that you are always nearby.

I'll be seeing you...

Chapter 8

HEAVEN on EARTH

*When the angels turn the lights on in heaven
tonight and hang out the stars in the blue, when
you see that first star through your window
tonight, I'll be dreaming my darlin of you.....*

The Angel Song, Curt Massey

Little Book Cliffs
Grand Junction, Colorado
Morning/Night, August

To Mochi
Backyard in the Sky
Dear Sweetheart,

Once again, we climbed back into the car. I noticed how comfortable the back seat was as we drove down the end of the mountain. Whether Peter or Flo, seated up front, were disappointed by not seeing any mustangs was difficult to determine since they engaged in another focused topic about her house and garden weeds.

I felt animated by the sight of the basset hound and sensed that their weed conversation had finished. I decided to tell them about the time you and I sat in our backyard one summer night.

"Would you like to hear a story about my backyard?" I called out to my two friends in the front seat.

"I'd love to hear it," Flo responded.

"Sure," chimed in Peter.

The sky darkened. I closed my eyes. It helped retrieve the story from my mind. I loved to reminisce. Dusk set in on a hot July night and you were lying on the brick deck in our backyard. Seeing you from behind I had an irresistible urge to get down and hug you. When you felt my arms around you, you immediately stood up. Just as quickly you sat down again continuing to look out into the backyard. Determined to hug you, I sat down next to you and once again put my arms around you. This time you did not move.

Gently pulling you toward me,
we sat facing the center of the yard several feet from an old stake that supported a laundry line. Although the backyard always felt like a safe

46

place, at night it became mysterious. Bushes encircled its perimeter. The trunk of the large maple tree on the right darkened while on the left, the Christmas tree branches became a large awning. Whenever it rained you took shelter under it to safely conduct business. We huddled together as the light disappeared and darkness eased in.

Looking upward at the early evening sky always amazed me. Another world was out there. It seemed so far away, yet so near.
Feeling the fur on your long ears brush against my head, I watched as the stars followed by the moon became visible. They lit up the sky. Even though stars are magical, I was drawn to the strange caverns of the moon, dark, deep and distant. Feeling your ears twitch, I returned to earth. When I looked over at you, I was surprised to see that you too were looking up at the moon and the stars.

I marveled at the moon's caverns. Our astronauts have walked the moon's surface. Even affluent civilians are not far behind following in their path, trying to bring that satellite into our global environment. There was something so dark and distant about this sphere that led me to wonder how it came into being in the first place. Why was it there? How did the caverns form their shapes?

Although the moon seems to be standing still it was actually moving, circling the earth once a month. I often wonder who made up the schedule. And the stars, spreading out along the immense sky felt so far away, yet felt so close. How did each star get to where it was?

The answer was more a feeling than a thought. A powerful force with not only an infinite mind but brilliant creativity was in control, a force greater than anything found on earth. Little by little, looking at this other world, I became aware that the powerful force in the universe above was the same in the backyard with you and me. It was not accidental that the roots from the maple tree on our right were created from the soil of the ground, just as it was not an accident that the fur tree on our left had long droopy branches with little brown cones that fell to the ground and made seeds. The darkness was no longer scary but surrounded us with love, a love that produced a perfectly balanced world, moving at tremendous speed with absolute precision.

Our little world took on a new meaning. I was no longer just an observer, seated, looking out from my vantage point on the deck. The earth was under the concrete deck holding it in place, supporting the brick steps we sat on. The roots from the trees gave the earth strength. Just as the sky came down to merge with the trees, I merged with the night. No longer looking out at the backyard, I was part of the backyard, part of the universe, even if a tiny part, limited only by my imagination.

Then the moon, stars, trees and ground stopped being physical objects. Rather they became the images and symbols for the entity behind them. They became distinct expressions of an original Mind with endless capabilities. An infinite Mind created it all. A boundless Mind contained it all at the same time. An unending Mind managed all of creation. This was not the first time I got a peek behind the dark forms of what appeared to be.

I could sense a loving Spirit moving underneath, behind, around and through everything close by; in the backyard and far away, in the air up to the sky, and the universe beyond.

"It has to be God!" I whispered to myself. "Who else could it be? Who else could provide such sights and inspire such feelings? God in the universe seemed natural, but God here in the backyard, in our little world seemed natural too. If

God is in the air I am breathing, I must be part of that creation too. We all must be part of it! All of humanity, the environment and the cosmos are connected as one. Linked together, part of the same heavenly design, we are all dependent on each other to be whole. God is everywhere!"

I felt your ears twitch again. You sat up and looked directly at me with a keen look in your eyes, ready to speak. Although no sound or voice came from your throat, I heard you clearly. It was your mind to my mind, a special language that did not need sound or movement.

"So, you figured out that you are part of the great universe. That's nice. But what about me, where do I fit in? Where do all the other dogs and animals fit in? Not only pets like me but farm animals, wild animals and sea animals? Are we not part of the same universe God created under the same loving Divine direction? Or do you humans have special rights the rest of us are denied?"

"Typical, just like you, to make things complicated on a relaxing night, Mochi. If you had asked me when first met you, I would have said, yes with reservations. You and all the animals on the earth are certainly part of creation but whether you are kindred to God or under His same direction is another matter. If a vote were taken today, history and the consensus would be no. Despite challenges and growing animal compassion awareness, the prevailing opinion is that animals were created for the benefit of humans."

And speaking for the side of those who divide life into human beings and secondary forms of life, I must ask; "What are you dogs and the rest of the animals, pets, farmed or wild doing on the earth anyway? Besides those we can eat, milk, exhibit, ride, use in a rodeo, research, or for some other benefit, what is your purpose? Are any of you really essential? We, humans, do all the important things that are necessary to control the world. If you did contribute anything to our way of life, we could even make substitutes."

Of course, I did not say anything like this to you because I knew I would never get away with it. Not when you looked at me or rather through me with those keen x-ray brown eyes of yours as you did tonight. Also, after living with you, I no longer felt that way about your relatives.

Once more you spoke in your silent but stirring way and what I understood was, "Just how essential or indispensable everything is in this life, in this universe, is not for any human to decide. The Creator decides. Humans are too superficial for such limitless power. And besides you, humans are confused about the meaning of existence.

What is so confusing?" Mochi persisted. "Truth is hidden from you, because you chose to look down at the universe from where you consider is your rightful elevated place, through arrogance and conceit. To see and understand the universe you should view it from the inside, as part of the whole. The universe simply cannot be segregated into parts. If you humans are part of this whole, connected to the Creator, then so are we animals. If you are part of this unending plan, so are we."

Mochi continued in her penetrating way, "We are all in this together. I need you and you need me. We need each other. We can only help each other if we live in the Creator's everlasting presence as one, as a part of it."

You gave my chin a couple of licks, wagged your tail frantically and bounded down the stairs with those short legs of yours heading for our backyard. You made your statement. I stood up and followed you into the darkness of the yard as an enlightened, better person.

Relating all this to Flo and Peter from the back seat, took a little more time than writing this letter. By the time I finished, we descended the mountain and were back on Coal Canyon Road almost halfway home. Flo and Peter neither asked any questions nor spoke to each other about their boring topics as they usually did when they drove. I questioned if they both indulged in a little deep thinking. I believe so.

After returning to Flo's house and thinking back over the events of the day on the mountain, I wondered if my attempt to communicate with the horses through the universe connected me with you instead. It had to be more than a coincidence to come across a basset hound on an isolated rough terrain mountain at 8 a.m. Did you help the lab find us, to bring us to the basset? Did you try to make me feel better?

I know you are always looking after me.

I'll be seeing you...

Chapter 9

NATIVES

In the beginning God created the heavens and the earth; the earth was waste and void; darkness covered the abyss, and the spirit of God was stirring above the waters.

The Story of Creation

Ouray, Colorado
Morning, August

To Mochi
Backyard in the Sky
Dear Sweetheart,

The day after we returned from Little Book Cliffs, Flo announced that Peter's brother, Dennis, was taking his two dogs, Siobhan and Poppy, for a walk along the creek on the way to Ouray. Named after Chief Ouray of the Utes, a Native American tribe, the town was a little under an hour's drive from Grand Junction.

Raised in Colorado like his brother, Dennis was an extremely quiet man. Although unlike his brother, who lived a fairly conventional life as an accountant after serving in the Navy, Dennis enjoyed being independent and lived somewhat off the grid.

At the time of my visit, Dennis and his two dogs were living with Peter. Not wanting to impose on his brother, Dennis, Siobhan, and Poppy went on frequent walks and outings. On this day Dennis had decided to take a drive and walk along a canal on the way to Ouray. He invited Flo to join him. Since I was a guest, I was included.

Mid-morning, a Chevy truck with Dennis behind the wheel rolled into Flo's driveway carrying two Wheaton terriers in the back seat secured behind a screen. Flo climbed into the front first, and settled in the middle seat next to Dennis, while I climbed in second and sat by the window. Seated three across, I felt like I was back in high school. The Wheatons were close by on the other side of the screen. Although it was another truck, this vehicle felt cozier than the one of the previous day. Perhaps it was because we sat huddled in the front seat, or perhaps we were not driving up any steep mountains, or maybe because there was no endless banter between Flo and Dennis. For whatever reason, our little gang made their way onto the freeway toward Ouray. I glanced at the two dogs. Somehow Wheaton terriers did not seem to fit a rough and tumble man like Dennis. How did they come together? Before I could ask, Dennis surprisingly spoke up.

"Siobhan and Poppy lived with a woman who enjoyed her Irish heritage; consequently, she named her first dog, Siobhan. In Gaelic, it means God is gracious as this woman was. The dog's owner and her husband retired and relocated to Grand Junction from the East Coast. She was 92 when she died, leaving behind her 95-year-old husband, who had no interest in caring for the two dogs.

Before departing," Dennis continued, "she requested that the dogs not be separated. Siobhan was fearless while Poppy was shy and retiring. Without Siobhan, Poppy would be lost. A friend from a nearby church, who knew my dog Critter had just died, asked if I wanted to adopt. Critter was a rangy mute and loved the outdoors. We enjoyed our hikes together. The Wheatons seemed a little too New York for me. Siobhan and Poppy were Dude Ranch type dogs with their whiskers groomed into mustaches. I could easily see them wearing bow ties.

Afraid of what could happen to these two guys, I took them," Dennis explained.

"I've never regretted it."

For a man who rarely spoke, he certainly was finding his words. The story of losing your dog and then finding a new one, or perhaps two, is a story that even the quietest person needs to tell.

Flo laughed at the story while I politely said; "How nice of you to take them."

With the truck windows open, I felt the temperature rise. Siobhan and Poppy, no doubt felt it too. Predictions were again for 100 degrees. From the windows, I saw farmland and an occasional ranch. Even a Dude Ranch mentioned by Dennis seemed in the middle of nowhere. One of the dogs, Poppy, seemed to sense my mind wandering and pushed his nose through the part of the screen near my head, bringing me back to our adventure. Dennis pulled into a small unpaved parking lot. Maybe it was the sound of gushing water that stirred Poppy and not my thoughts. We had arrived at the canal.

We humans stepped out of the truck to the sound of bubbling water and birds chirping. When Dennis opened the door of the cargo area, Siobhan jumped out while Poppy waited to be guided out. Reaching in, Dennis pulled out a brown leash for

Siobhan and a pink one for Poppy. What seemed like a trace of embarrassment passed over his face while he fastened the pink leash on Poppy.

"The leash came with her," he felt the need to explain. "It was probably bought by her owner, who no doubt pampered the two of them."

Unlike yesterday's trip to Little Book Cliffs, this landscape was totally flat. The canal, which to me looked like a small river with a strong current, was bordered on the far side by a wooded area and on the side where we stood by a dirt path. Next to the dirt path was some overgrowth whose shoreline came to a larger body of water, perhaps a lake.

Dennis released Siobhan on the downward slope of the path, while he held onto Poppy's pink leash. Siobhan ran freely ahead of us along the side of the trail that bordered the canal, enjoying the walk better than all of us. Excited, she moved easily along the area that inclined toward the canal. Elevated, she could see more. Tail wagging it was clear that she had more fun than her human companions.

Poppy too was not left out of the gaiety. The woods were filled with birds singing as if part of a huge choir in the sky. Amazed she looked up and all around. Perhaps their high-pitched chirping resonated with the dog's hearing ability.

From our time together, I understood the ecstatically frantic behavior of Siobhan and Poppy. Although the canal provided some moisture, it was still a hot morning. However, the heat did not bother our two friends or slow them down. Their secret was what I learned from being close to you. They do not seek adventure; they are the adventure. They carry their happiness inside them and pour it out over everything. Their inner eagerness carries them forward expecting to find good.

Running ahead on the path, Siobhan frequently darted back to check on us, letting us know she cared about our whereabouts. Maybe she felt sorry for us not being able to keep up with her. Although Poppy did not run, she too showed her excitement with her upturned head, cup-like floppy ears and wagging tail. Although not young dogs, their energy was continual along with their delight and appreciation for being alive. They were inspirational.

It is just like you dogs to live in the moment and find amusement and contentment out of very little. Living completely in the present with your entire being, no halfhearted holding back only strengthened the adventure.

Siobhan ran close to the canal while Poppy walked closer to us on the far overgrown side, each with heads bobbing, sniffed everything that came their way from the air to flowers along the path. Although the canal offered no cooling breeze, they did not seem to mind.

Dennis pointed toward the woods where two deer stared at us. One was bigger and appeared to be the mother while the smaller her fawn. The fawn reclined in the grass while the mother stood. Both their coats were a very light tan and I could see speckles on the mother's back. Keeping our steady pace, they did not move. Siobhan had long since passed their line of sight. Perhaps the deer did not run away because we were quiet, fitting into their environment rather than them into ours.

Now let me tell you a little about the deposition of Dennis. He was an expert at listening to people, animals and the environment. You would have liked him.

From Flo, I learned how from early childhood the American Indians of the Southwest had fascinated him. He became a landscape artist.

His affluent clients with large properties kept his business afloat. Not surprising for an outdoors enthusiast, he used native colors, designs and materials in his projects.

His lifestyle was simple and quiet. He spoke very little. Now a recently retired widower with grown children, he spent much of his time with nature as his companion, where speech was not necessary.

Not only did Dennis use Southwestern materials in his designs, but he was well versed in the history of the era. Though I received most of my understanding of the Southwest by watching Gene Autry and the Lone Ranger on TV, Dennis learned through reading, traveling the area and meeting local people of Native American heritage.

The Utes lived in the area of Colorado I was visiting. Flo, having spent so much time living in the area shared her extensive knowledge of the Utes. These Native Americans had a unique relationship with the environment, giving and taking
from the earth. They felt there was no separation between them and the land. They were part of it. They did not own the land— the land owned them.

Flo said the Utes ate meat only in the winter when they could not grow grain. They were free, with their own internal organization or government. They traveled by foot to locations of water, the central component for plants as well as animals. These locations became their campgrounds. The land took care of them.

The Utes people were content and spiritually minded, but the advent of civilization brought them much suffering. Spanish conquistadors used them as slaves, while white men consumed the land and placed them on reservations. The early American government had its own view of land ownership.

Flo presented an interesting thought: What if the Native Americans had conquered the White man? Civilization also brought infectious diseases. Due to the limited number of people in the Native American group culture, they could not buildup any immunity. If we did not have all the technological advances we have today, perhaps our life spans would be shorter, but maybe our lives would be happier with more contentment.

If the Native Americans had won, they may also have changed the course of history concerning the treatment of African Americans. They may have had no use for slaves. Their perception of being part of the land would have been inconsistent for importing others to live there. Flo was certainly a free thinker.

Flo described Dennis as one of the most religious people she knew. Being a churchgoer, I thought his religious tendency would mean he would come to church with us on Sunday. That was not the case. Although he and his brother were raised as Christians, the last time Dennis was in a church was when his grandfather died, about 50 years ago. It amused me that although he did not attend church, it did not stop him from driving his friends without transportation to church. He was constantly aware of the Spirit and strived to live in balance with it. Recently taking up the hobby of wire art which seemed a good fit for his hands-on skills, his major motivation was reducing waste by re-purposing to preserve the environment.

Dennis is a grateful man who according to Flo prays mainly by giving thanks, rarely asking for favors or his own special intentions. She told me about his prayer routine. If he needed guidance, he would 'sit with the Lord.' Before attempting to communicate with the Spirit, he quieted his mind by emptying it of thoughts, attempting to make it blank. Although he does not fast before these sessions, he overindulges in neither food nor beverage. His diet does not include alcohol. Many times, he works out before these sessions so his physical body is also relaxed. He then goes to a distant peaceful place like the mesa or if travel is not convenient, he goes to a quiet space in Peter's backyard, where he opens himself to the universe.

Unrushed and subdued, he trustingly listens for the Spirit to talk to him giving guidance and instructions. His favorite time for prayer is early morning when it is easiest to clear his mind. His religious practices, or rather lack of formal practices, moved him toward the Spirit. Flo also told me about his uncanny ability to sense the spirits and hearts of people and animals.

Suddenly Dennis shouted to Siobhan, who was quite a way ahead of us, to return to the fold. I watched in amazement as Siobhan turned around, looked over her shoulder at Dennis and returned to his side.

"Is something wrong?" I asked him. Following the direction of Dennis's arm, as he pointed down the trail, I saw a large snake slither across it.

"How did you know the snake was

coming?"

"I felt its presence," he said matter-of-factually. "With a proper attitude, snakes need not be feared, but with the dogs being so rambunctious today, they might have been startled by the snakes or the snakes might have been startled by the dogs." He further explained, "Siobhan and Poppy are also still new to the common creatures of the West."

Dennis's feelings about the snake were certainly accurate. In private, I talked to Flo a little more about his intuition. Was the sudden presence in the small mind of something from the Big Mind usually so reliable?

"He definitely is in touch with some other forces because he is usually aware of things we can't see and he is amazingly on target," she replied.

"Do you think God is involved? Could God be speaking to him?"

"Not only is God speaking to him but he listens," she said.

I'll be seeing you...

Chapter 10

DEER FRIENDS

Grand Junction, Colorado
Afternoon, August

To Mochi
Backyard in the Sky
Dear Sweetheart,

When our walk along the canal ended and the parking area came into view, I once again thought about Dennis' feelings toward snakes. He didn't seem afraid of them but rather regarded them as some sort of fellow being that had the right to travel on the same road he was traveling. He considered what the snake could be feeling as well as the feelings of fellow travelers, Siobhan and Poppy.

Dennis was able to navigate the three. Although he did not go in the path of the snake, I had a feeling the snake would not have bothered him. The reptile may have had regard for his fellow traveler too.

In this part of the country, there are more

snakes than where we came from but the long-standing hatred, bordering on panic, of the animal exists in both places. However even in our part of the country, like Dennis, snakes and other wild animals didn't scare you either, did they?

I remember the day you sauntered into the backyard for your first early morning outing while I was in the kitchen boiling water for my first cup of tea. As I turned to look out the window of our back door, I saw a deer standing under the large fir tree beside you. In a panic, I grabbed two pots, ready to make a loud noise to frighten the animal away. Clutching the pots, I rushed outside. The second before I started banging, I saw that you were both standing perfectly still, neither of you moving into the other's space. You looked at one another with surprise and awe, sending signals of respect, neighborly understanding, and maybe even a "good morning." A playful look appeared in your eyes, when the deer shook her head, bobbed her tail, turned, and quickly walked toward the back of the yard finding her way out. There was no need to proceed with my New Year's Eve percussion rendition.

There are even old Native American folktales about how snakes struck the White man but did not attack the Indian. The slithering creature's century-old stinging skin choice is well known though not understood. Most White men had not even the slightest idea why snakes had such selective animosity. Nor is it clear how the snake could tell the two apart.

White men took precautions against snakes by wearing high boots and arming themselves with guns. In the Old West, a weapon was used against almost everyone and everything as needed. They paid attention to where they walked and what they touched with their hands. They carefully considered their behavior towards the creature.

Native Americans on the other hand did just the opposite. They behaved casually toward snakes, wearing light moccasins or no shoes at all. They carried knives, generally used as a tool, not a weapon. Their hands moved freely. Although easy targets for striking fangs, the reptiles chose to direct their assaults at the high-booted, well-armed, White men.

The morning you met the deer in our back yard you were not frightened of your visitor. Rather you had finished your daily morning business and were walking around happily under your favorite tree when she appeared. I, on the other hand, at the sight of her, armed myself with pots and pans ready to cause a ruckus.

Why did the snakes act so violently toward the White men and leave the Native American Indians alone? Why did the deer seem so undisturbed by you? Dennis knows why the Native Americans and snakes were on such peaceable terms. I do too. After watching you for so many years, I know why you and the deer were good neighbors. Although the reason is a simple one, its effects are powerful! It can be, I believe, a source or solution for every worry that frustrates and confuses humans today whether an individual or a community. The reason is simple; it is just two easy words, *mental attitudes*.

The White man taught to fear snakes had his own attitude while the legendary American Indian held a wholly different one. Fear became hate. Civilization brought fear and hate together teaching the White man to kill any snake on sight. The Native American was raised to be in harmony with all forms of life, including animal.

The reptile was a form of creation that moved about on the same plain as he. Other forms such as the snake, although different according to the Indian's upbringing, deserved the same freedoms of life, liberty and pursuit of happiness as he did. The Native American has neither fear nor dislike of snakes, and hardly ever hurts them. Just as he travels about conducting his own life, he respects the snake's right to do the same.

A difference in mental attitude may seem unimportant, but in many cases determines the outcome of fear or acceptance and even life or death. Legend tells us the snake is aware of the difference in feelings between the White man and the Native American.

Although on the surface it looks like the snake attacks the White man's physical body, what he is really attacking is his hateful attitude. Without hate, it is doubtful that the White man's physique would disturb the snake. The snake's poison is pitted against the poison in the White man's heart, not his body.

The two wage an endless war against each other which neither has ever won. Fear, that common emotion often coupled with violent feelings makes both snakes and humans highly dangerous. The snake returns the human's hostility with hostility; his ferocity with ferocity; his aimed gun with aimed venom. And so it continues and will probably not change till the White man has a conversion of heart. When he removes the fear and hate from his mind and soul and replaces it with an understanding of the value of his universe and the creatures in it, his change of heart could happen.

What was I so afraid of that morning? Possibly the deer hurting you? The unknown? However, my fears never materialized. On the other hand, you did not seem to be frightened by the deer while she in turn did not seem to be a bit disturbed by you, maybe even a little amused. Perhaps knowing she was not harmful, you wanted to play with her. While she, realized that you were not aggressive, she was not interested in your games, and simply turned and walked away. A lot of communication took place between the two of you in a very short time.

What would the deer have done if I came out banging my pots? Would she have turned and run? Not an aggressive animal she probably would have. Yes, probably run through anything in her path, like my new herb garden.

In a much less dramatic way my mental attitude toward the deer, similar to the contrast between the White man and the snake, was very different from yours. Perhaps you saved me only from a trampled flower bed but the lesson was still the same and has always remained with me.

Mental attitudes make a difference and until they change nothing changes.

Approaching with suspicion, anger and fear, creates suspicion, anger and fear in the other being as well till they feel the need to flee, defend or attack. Isn't that how a suspicious or hateful attitude works, whether you are approaching a deer in your backyard or a peaceful protester on the sidewalk? Violence can erupt. Isn't this how violence starts?

Where does a suspicious and hateful attitude come from? How does it develop? What keeps it going? Is hating the opposite of loving or is hate, fear turned on itself? Does it come from meeting people who are different from you; a different skin color, culture, religion, political party or sexual preference, whether they are in your backyard, neighborhood, school, office, factory, farm or even family!

Growing up I saw many riots on TV. They all seemed to start with usually unarmed people carrying placards coming out in public *en masse* confronted by law enforcers armed with clubs, guns and even attack dogs. Not only did the two sides carry diverse equipment but they carried different attitudes. As time went by with societal changes, including the lack of gun control, frequently protesters carried guns and were confronted by even more guns. Our increasingly violent equipment matches our increasingly violent attitudes.

How can peaceful protesting change a condition? Is it the people that protesters move against or is it their attitudes? These struggles between protesters and law enforcement, humans and animals will continue, I suppose, until hatred and anger are no longer in control, and humans learn to appreciate and respect all of creation.

Mochi, that morning you changed my perception of deer. Passing through our back yard, deer never did any damage to you or my property. I am always grateful to you for your example and your sometimes baffling and amusing ability to help me be aware of my mental attitudes particularly when I am in the presence of humans or animals that are different from me.

If only I had known this years ago, I would have been able to better appreciate not only people who don't look or think like me but also animals whether pets, livestock or in the wild. I thought and felt more like the White man. Now, thanks to you, I think and feel more like the Native

American Indian.

Humans have an intuitive ability to be in touch with the feelings and thoughts of others but rarely use it as a common practice. They generally regard it as coming from low intellect, the occult or even instability. Even with a rise in the popularity of complementary therapies along with the increasing presence of animal communicators, Therapeutic Touch, REIKE and yoga practitioners, although all highly regarded, are still considered out of the mainstream. Even though they may be making progress, creeping into conventional medicine, they still belong to a small circle surrounded by doubt and suspicion.

You were not influenced by any of these barriers, were you? I believe no one, including me, ever fooled you for very long. Your uncanny ability to hear not only what a person said, but to penetrate the heart it was coming from, was never known to fail.

Our society relies on saying one thing while thinking another. As long as our behavior is socially acceptable, we give ourselves the license to think and feel one thing while we do another. Covering up real feelings leads to smiling at people while we privately hate them, compete with them, discredit them or minimize them. Yes, we humans have the exceptional quality to generate the only two-faced, two-tongued, two feeling and two-timing beings to walk on the earth: Behavior your four-legged relatives would never condone.

But as long as there are genuine people like Dennis and Flo and dogs like you who acted and lived as good examples of honesty and sincerity, being your true self, there is still hope for all of us.

I'll be seeing you....

Chapter 11

DOGS RULE

Princeton, New Jersey
Evening, August

To Mochi
Backyard in the Sky
Dear Sweetheart,

The Colorado adventure is over. Flo settled into her house in Grand Junction now that her mother moved to your eternal neighborhood. Dennis packed up his truck, left his brother Peter, and headed to the South East to catch up with his grandchildren. For me, it was time to go back East.

After divergent expeditions, back in our little cape cod in Princeton, New Jersey, the world news came into full scary view. According to the online news, TV stations from both sides of the aisle, radio and friends chatter both on the internet and in person, the country and the world were in a bad place for human conditions. Anger, bitterness, frustration and discontent exist everywhere, with corruption, greed and violence unchecked.

Dishonesty is the norm. Social and moral values are left by the wayside. The domestic and global atmosphere is irresponsible, inhumane and unintelligent. To put it simply, the world is in chaos.

I am embarrassed to confess this to you, an animal, a dog, but it is the truth! Our country appears divided on how to proceed. The world suffers from the same divisiveness. People here seem to forget we fought one civil war to stay together! Many deem our country hopeless. They want to leave but are finding it difficult to find a place to go since the whole world is upside down.

Can you believe such things are happening to us humans? We who are the superior beings, who have dominion over the earth and all its creatures, should be stewards of the environment. Can this be happening to us, supposedly self-righteous people? And then there is our country, the world's leading civilization for over a century. Yes, we whose mantra is defending and protecting the rights and well-being of our fellow humans. Instead of loving our neighbor, we many times go after them and their property with calculated ruthlessness that no other lower animal would consider doing.

It is easy for everyone to agree that something needs to change, and everyone has a solution as to what should be done. However, most of the remedies focus on reforming the other guy, group, rabble-rousers or another country. It never crosses their minds to look at the behavior of their guys, their group, their rabble-rousers or their country. They act as if they never heard the principle that to make a change, we have to start with ourselves and what is in our own hearts.

From my perspective, the situation is not as bad as it is being broadcasted. We humans have without a doubt lost our moral compass, social wisdom and spiritual direction! The cause? In my opinion, it is because we keep ourselves constantly busy, so we have no time to experience our intimate thoughts and feelings.

We have lost touch with our better selves, our true values. What would help us are improved relationships with the animals of the ground, birds of the air, fish of the sea, trees and plants, and any other overlooked friends, all of which offer garden-fresh wisdom. Rather than reinvent, we create for the first time, a relationship with these neighbors we were previously unaware of.

Is it even possible this late in the game for

us humans to regain a simpler happier world, the world we may have known as children? Who could possibly help accomplish this?

Our guides should not be other humans, who got us there in the first place. How do we find qualified guides? We need to travel outside of ourselves. No need to go far, just beyond our human species. If you will indulge me in wonderland, I imagine animals, especially dogs like you, should be included in learning institutions. Farm animals, wild species, jungle animals and marine life could also assist in the curriculum, but you canines would be the main educators. Give dogs the ability to train humans rather than the other way around.

The art of listening as well as giving a good bark, faithfulness, living in the moment, gratefulness for all you receive, calmness, keeping your head, utter joy, clowning around, ecstatic movement, compassion, empathy, danger alerts and giving and sharing love are some of the many things you canines could teach us, humans.

Schools could be established or courses could be developed and added to the curriculum in already existing institutions. The main difference would be that dogs are the teachers and humans are the students.

There could be a Bachelor of Arts degree in Companionship with a concentration in Listening. This was one of your best attributes. Other courses could develop faithfulness, kindness, consideration, understanding, and constancy. Perhaps a Visual Performing Arts Degree in being a Clown. You always provided me with at least a laugh a day.

Labs would make good instructors for the Clown 101 course since they, next to you bassets, are some of the goofiest dogs. We humans need to laugh more. For Health Care Professionals dogs could provide courses in self-health, eating regular meals and getting plenty of exercise. You never complained when you were sick. And don't forget Alternative Health. No one like you dogs can teach us how to de-stress by making time for smelling the flowers, rolling in the grass or letting frustrations out with a good bark.

Although this may sound like a novel idea, it is not far off from what schools and libraries have started by offering time for students to read to dogs. Service dogs are also in schools now to give students with allergies peanut alerts as well as offer moral support.

However, my proposal differs in one very important way, dogs will not be in a subordinate role but assume a leadership position. How will they lead? How will they teach? By example! It is innate in them. No need for lectures, power point presentations or reading/writing assignments.

Conveying these characteristics is an art. Since your canine relatives naturally possess these attributes, they can easily pass them on.

What would this program look like? It would be individualized, just as students vary possessing different abilities. The learner could be any age. Each human student would be matched with their own dog educator. The instruction would take place wherever they came together. It could be an open-air classroom such as on a beach or high up on a mountain. A place of easy access would also do nicely such as a quiet safe neighborhood street or your own backyard.

The student would be instructed not to talk but to watch and listen. Being completely quiet aids in developing the ability to receive. If the trainee has a favorite breathing exercise to clear the mind, which in turn has been found to stimulate the imagination and promote creativity, it would be encouraged.

To solidify the process, the student is advised to carry a notebook and pencil. If they insist on an electronic device, it should be one that does not connect to the internet. In this way, there is no temptation for distractions, such as online shopping. Since no textbooks would be required for this course, the notebook is essential. To further facilitate the process, if the students are willing, repurposed clothes could be worn. Garments from loved ones who the learner wishes to remember are well suited here, not only to fully utilize what we have but to inspire. This tribute to a person who has passed both inspires and empowers with lessons and stories from another time even from another generation.

The student, notebook in hand, would follow close behind the canine educator to mindfully observe and record all that seemed important. Later the student would review the notes to determine if the information noted expanded knowledge and furthered the progress of becoming a better person in this world.

The students' progress would be measured: Notice that any reference to test or exam is omitted. Instead, they would be required to list all the good qualities recognized in the dog professor. If you are more comfortable with the word test, it could be sort of an open-book exam. Some folks also need every course to have a book. In this course, the book is the notebook. For this assignment, the student would be allowed to use the internet or any hard copy source that listed synonyms describing personal character strengths.

The results might be surprising: The list might be longer than expected! Our educational explorers should take the opportunity to absorb these traits. My guess is students will be in for a big surprise! Our explorer would then be requested to list their own finest attributes, match them to those of the dog professor and make an honest comparison. In this way, light would be shed on which of the two made the best use of their good qualities in their usual day-to-day activities during their limited time on earth.

Once I tried this exercise on you, Mochi. Your curiosity and playfulness always intrigued me, but I thought you were in your own puppy dog place so to speak, making your attributes dog-like.

Surprise, surprise, your list not only was longer than mine but had qualities like courage and acceptance that did not show up on my list of supposedly human attributes! It took me some time to process that not only you specifically, but your canine relatives in general, possessed high qualities. It was inspiring that you not only possessed the qualities themselves, which would have been enough but that you were committed to them at all times, never wavering, regardless of the circumstances. It was truly an eye-opening exercise for me. From that day forward I looked at you and your canine relatives differently, not to mention how I saw myself. The exercise illuminated my own life and showed me some things about myself I needed to know.

Having dogs as teachers will open the eyes of many of their human students. Any dog from any breed or mixed breeds would be a great teacher. The average man or woman or even child for that matter would agree that dogs are stress busters offering unlimited amounts of companionship. Most would also agree that a relationship with a dog can make us a better person.

The goal of this wonderland would just expand the good work. Adults are always looking for new and innovative ways to teach. Why not try this approach? It would definitely be fun and since both our young and mature learners look at life differently, dogs may offer a common teaching ground. It is also only fair to give you canines a try since you have been our subordinates for so long. Although we have enlisted you in some rewarding service areas, what else have we, the supposedly more advanced species, taught you about life? We have made you our pets, trackers, guards, hunters or personal slaves. Humans rarely take into consideration that you have attributes that with help could make our lives and yours worthwhile beyond our imagination.

What a terrific teacher you were and still are today. You never went to college or even graduated from high school. You were an animal or just a dog, but your presence only brought good things to everyone. You influenced others while they were not conscious of it.

Comforting people, as well as other animals in pain and fear while relieving everyday stress, you enabled them to live simpler, freer and happier lives. You opened hardened hearts allowing love to come in: You inspired people to do things that made them feel good about themselves. You helped them on their journey toward the infinite.

And you imparted countless other lessons while empowering and offering comfort which you

did with your sweet and loving personal example!
What more could be asked of an educator?

I'll be seeing you...

Chapter 12

VOYAGERS

Inside Passage, Alaska
Afternoon, September

To Mochi
Backyard in the Sky
Dear Sweetheart,

     I am traveling North to Alaska on a cruise ship.

Rolled up in a blanket, I was lying in a lounge chair on the deck surrounded by fellow shipmates to my right and left. Suddenly from the direction of the rail, a friendly male voice called out, "baby whale." My fellow hearties and I jumped up and rushed to the rail just in time to see far below us a tiny whale taking little scooping dives into the choppy waves. I felt so afraid for this tiny animal that seemed so fragile in the rough Pacific Ocean, yet he was holding his own moving along the waves not appearing to tire. When our ship passed by and the whale could no longer be seen, we all returned to our chairs to continue soaking up the sun. Looking out over the ocean, other than the waves the ship churned up, the Pacific, true to its name, had just a slight movement.

We sailed toward Glacier Bay, the focal point of our journey. Although there were close to 2,000 people on board the ocean liner, staff included, up to now we were one big congenial community. The group included a knitting club of about 50 people, of which I was a member. We explored each port of call and returned to the ship when "All Aboard" was called. Travelers' enthusiasm contributed to friendly interactions on board.

During the first week of our voyage my fellow shipmates, coming from different parts of the country: the Pacific North West, California Coast, Midwest Heartland and the East Coast including New Jersey, with different political, social and I soon to find out scientific views, were able to graciously put regional beliefs aside. Any biased opinions soon fell by the wayside.

While walking through Juno with a couple of friends I made on board the ship, a woman from our knitting circle, recognized that we belonged to her group and were not interested in where her friends were headed, had asked if she could walk with us. The four of us strolled down the sidewalk through the town as old girl friends. We peered into the Red Dog Saloon, absorbed the old mining town atmosphere, browsed through a modern-day yarn shop, and when she felt she had traveled far enough she casually returned to her fold. It was a comfortable relaxed community. The common interest in knitting united four strangers to enjoy an afternoon of fun even without knitting.

But this morning we dis-entwined ourselves from one another and moved back into our regional stance on locations, politicians and medicines.

Even my knitting circle retreated from its original show of congeniality. The friendly smiles and good morning greetings experienced when entering the elaborate breakfast buffet were replaced with empty stares and silence.

Relationships are a mystery and yet we humans remove the mystery by adding our convenient wants. When it is in our best interest, we form them and when the connections, encompassing friendship, family, marriage, work, church, office, neighborhood, and travel, no longer exist for us we break them. Even today's new type of relationship-- online friends and followers is handled in the same way. We drift in and out as it suits us. Our ability to form and sustain relationships has always been a question. Now online communication causes us to ask even more questions. The answers to either face-to-face or virtual type of relationships seem to revolve around the idea that we humans want convenience, not consistency.

The mystery of relationships whether between individuals who live in our home or across vast borders continues to be explored. One idea is that we know what to do to sustain our connections but we lack the ability or choose not to use our ability to stay connected. There may be truth in these theories. However, I have seen firsthand that we humans have the ability to make a group experience fun, workable and enjoyable. The 2,000 people on board our ship, which included my knitting cohort, accomplished this every day during the first week of our cruise.

How did we do this? Not only my knitting cohort but the other 1,950 people from various US states and a few different countries with different levels of education, with an assortment of different political, religious, societal and even wellness perspectives adopted some basic attitudes. We used a canine live-in-the-moment philosophy! No cares, no worries and no memories of yesterday.

No obligations: No struggle over who would receive the most. We moved about with consideration for, and cooperation with each other.

We wanted to be happy and wanted others to be happy because we were happy. We stopped trying to impose our opinions on others about how the world should be run. In short, we stopped trying to run the world. Instead, we used the canine technique of taking whatever came our way and turned it into a playful adventure. No longer worried about what others would think, we did what we felt was right. In becoming our real selves, we discovered that we were wonderful people.

We saw the goodness in each other. It became easy to join together rather than stand behind our lines of separation. Spontaneous, we had a good time like children engaged in fun activities, good clean fun as we cruised along under the sun, the moon and the stars. Lighter than water, our outdoor /indoor fiesta moved forward inside our bubble.

That togetherness all came to an end last night when the World Wide Web broke our bubble with startling news. The information came through on the voyagers' cell phones, not from the ship's captain. As individual hearties got word, at first there was disbelief. Confusion soon followed as dueling media sites, brought news to the voyagers.

Headlines hurled us behind the scrimmage lines of our teams like football players lining up behind their quarterbacks ready for the next fierce play. Shock Headlines! Disregard for science...political interest ahead of life...awareness of danger but not sounding alerts...lies... suffering ...death...illusions to hide ignorance. Public, private and pious self-seekers leading the way, roping and tying officials into submission... cult-like behavior, manipulating state against state, group against group, and brother against sister.

A new virus appeared. Was it deadly? Was it no worse than a bad case of the flu? How did it spread? And the pivotal question for the hearties, was it on our ship? Questions we believed logically answered by doctors, researchers or our ship's captain. Instead, news alerts pointed in a different direction. Politics determined the virulence and spread of the disease.

A health condition was politicized by a country that was supposed to be advanced in every way, scientifically, socially and morally. The broadcasts sounded more like they were coming from a world over 200 years old when science had not advanced, and we were approaching a civil war. Not only did the entire unfolding of events surprise me but it embarrassed me. It was incredible to listen to what was happening in the world and to watch the behavior of my fellow voyagers.

After the media blitz of breaking news quieted down, our old identities came back and it was time to dis-entwine ourselves from each other and retreat into our little clans with similar if not unfounded beliefs. We came out to meet each other with common interests and social similarities and now we were going back behind our lines. Foolish? You would think we humans would have more sense, compassion and care for one's neighbor? The reason for this behavior pointed toward remembering where we came from. Our isolated feelings were promoted rather than educating us to reach out to each other as part of the universal plan we were living.

Those with open eyes could look up and see not only the neighbor in front of them but look out and beyond our immediate floating entertainment center and see a global world. Those aware of eternity, equipped with the ability to see the larger world could get a flash of the balance between the Master of the Universe and creation. A spiritual elevation might be needed to obtain that view.

The human has always had a difficult time understanding their place on the earth with accountability and responsibilities. Many would say we have only ourselves to blame. Humans practice looking at life through a small narrow lens, visualizing beautiful objects in front of them. If they believe these images to be true, he or she accepts life as a place to obtain more and more without any thought of impacting others who may want to be on a different road or ask what road they want to go down. Consequently, the human sees life through this narrow lens, constantly on the alert for those who might stand in the way of the accumulation of material objects and power. The human lives in fear of losing possessions, status and safety. Not surprisingly chaos follows.

Endeavoring to help the human comprehend that life is not a competition like races with horses, or placement in college courses, but rather an alliance of forces, challenged our leaders, education, religion, community, national, and global, for centuries. Although great strides have been made for race and gender, after viewing the events of the past few years it might even be said that we are going backwards. A peaceful world has never been attained. It might also be said that we humans lag behind animals in the wild, in the sea, on farms or in our homes.

It is my humble opinion, that we should take the lead from you dogs, as you showed me, and put aside our know-it-all arrogance, and exclusiveness and adopt your attitude toward life. It would be a big leap for our limited legs but we would land on solid ground. Imagine that one peaceful world of sharing life as an adventure with each other.

I'll be seeing you...

Photo by M. Cavallaro

Chapter 13

KINSHIP with CREATION

Glacier Bay, Alaska
Morning, September

To Mochi
Backyard in the Sky
Dear Sweetheart,

Our ship continued on its course to Glacier Bay, National Park. The captain advised we carry on with sanitizing our hands as much as possible and social distanced from each other. Buffet meals were staggered while tables were placed far apart. Ship restaurants proceeded to do the same. Entertainment events had attendee quotas. Deck chairs were spaced six feet apart. Although at this point it was not clear if masks were helpful, the captain advised they were ordered and on their way.

Why continue? The cruise line was not told by any authority that we could not proceed. At this point, very little was known either about the nature or the spread of the disease. No country-wide alarms were sounded nor guidance offered for the best course of action to take.

The captain reassured us that Alaska was a fairly safe place since it was believed the contagion had not yet reached that location, nor was there a large population to spread the disease among themselves or to visitors, by whatever means it was transmitted.

We were not trapped! If anyone wanted to leave, the ship's management would make arrangements to transport them. Like the rest of my hearties, I took the path of least resistance, decided to go along with the crowd, continue with the voyage and cruise to Glacier Bay. And what a cruise it was!

Sailing into the bay under the bright Alaskan sun we entered a different universe. My hearties flooded out on the deck as if an invisible undercurrent pulled us toward this watery heaven. I had forgotten what it was like to breathe clean air! Pure chilled air. However, my expectations of neat sheer crystal peaks were not met.

As our ship traveled closer, the glaciers came into view from a distance. When we looked up, we noticed a mass of brown coloring from the earth of the mountain mixed into the glacier. And when we lowered our gaze through the clearest of air, we saw the sparkle of the water under our floating hotel. Despite all the moisture, the air felt dry against my cheeks. From the corner of my eye, I saw my two shipmates, hearties standing beside me.

A young male voice came over the loudspeaker to give us a virtual tour. Surprisingly he did not call attention to the glaciers or the placid bay.

"We are fortunate to have this amazing view today. Feel the universe we are part of… clarity to eternity…flawless consciousness… kinship with creation." The calmness in his voice only heightened the peace.

It amazed me that a crew member could be so spiritual. No doubt he gave this speech often but there was no sign of mechanical delivery, only sincere reverence. The ship hovered as we absorbed the energy he described. While we stood on the deck, the windy air seemed to quiet down. Nothing interfered with our clarity and communing with nature.

My two hearties huddled together and returned to my awareness. Standing beside me, they inched closer to me. Since they hailed from New York, we immediately connected. They were NY strong as well as NY critical; continually pointing out things that were not up to the quality they anticipated. "The ship was not palatial enough; the knitting program was not organized enough." Nothing was enough. Now they too were totally quiet, mesmerized by the view and the voice over the loudspeaker.

"Today," the voice continued, "offers us a chance to watch the US National Park boat dock with our ship to let park rangers, board." From the coincidental vantage point on the deck, I watched as what looked like a tugboat appeared out of nowhere, and edged up to the side of our ocean liner. A man and a woman somehow oddly stepped from their rocking deck to what looked like the solid wall of our ship. The ladder was not visible to me. As the two disappeared on the ship, the little boat moved back and slowly sailed away. Eventually, we met the two visiting rangers in a reception room selling Glacier Bay memorabilia.

By now, the ship turned and pivoted in place giving us many opportunities to see the glaciers from different angles, without severing the spiritual connection with the universe. The visibility was too clear to lose us. The ice of the glaciers mixed into the brown earth of the mountain gave off a friendly rustic feeling rather than an intimidating one. Even from a distance, we saw the ice breaking off the mountain and heard its muffled sound when it plunged into the water. The NY Hearties moved to the rail to get a better view. One leaned over the siding while her sidekick anchored her waist.

Again, the voice continued; "Feel the serenity...simplicity...dignity and gratitude," followed by an enthusiastic deep breath. I took in a deep breath myself and noticed my two shipmates who had befriended me, had also moved and returned near me. I heard one say to the other; "We could use a little of this in New York."

The other responded, "Not so much the view but the feeling."

I saw an opening and chimed in; "What if you knew someone who could make you live those feelings every day?

"You know someone like that!" they both exclaimed.

"Yes. Her name is Mochi."

"Japanese? A Buddhist Monk?"

"She is an American. Most folks called her a dog."

I'll be seeing you...

The Three Wise Monkeys   Photo by M. Cavallaro

Chapter 14

MONKEY BUSINESS

"The message is the medium."

Marshall McLuhan

Nikko, Japan
Morning, October

To Mochi
Backyard in the Sky
Dear Sweetheart,

Since the disease had not yet touched Japan, and I was already in the Pacific, I decided hastily to continue my planned journey to the Land of the Rising Sun. Always concerned about my safety, you probably would have told me to go home.

On this trip, I traveled with a loose-knit tour group, led by a professional tour guide, a middle-aged Japanese woman. We affectionately called her Mama-San Suzie. She looked after us like a mother hen. Just the way I looked after you for 15 fulfilling years.

The tour visited many exotic places such as the sophisticated Tokyo, the more industrial Osaka and the artsy Kyoto. Although all different and unusual my favorite, and I believe it would have been yours too, was Nikko.

The town, a national park, about 100 miles from Tokyo, with its sacred shrines and temples is situated on a beautiful almost mysterious mountain.

The massive architecture and mix of colors were no ordinary sight. The blend of red, green and yellow was warm yet gave off a deep dark feeling.

We walked from our tour bus under giant

evergreen cryptomeria trees along wide paths. Remember the evergreen in our backyard you used to seek shelter under? The branches of this cryptomeria are not as long and have less of an overhang. The city is unquestionably a National Park displaying its shrines and temples out in the open amid the trees. You probably would not have liked the temples with their steep narrow steps. Your fear of heights in addition to your rhythmic way of bounding up steps might have easily tired you out, though you would have appreciated the park's mountainous landscape. It's a park where you could have walked out in the open area among the greenery. A perfect place for a dog like you who loved her daily walks. The people who lived on this holy mountain, not the tourists, were respectful in attitude and would have easily gained your seal of approval. It seemed fitting too for a holy city, a Toshogu Shrine, to be in a mountain closer to the Holy Spirit above us. Elevation gave off a sense of heaven and being near you.

We walked as a group up the narrow steep stairs of a fairly large Shinto temple. A monk appeared on the stairs. He held out his hand to help me. To gain a little more stability, grateful, I gently grasped it. There were no side rails to hold onto.

The temple was dark both on the outside and inside. Compared to the churches I knew, the floor space was empty. There were no pews. Instead, there were sacks of grain on the floor with Japanese words printed on them. This seemed out of place in a house of worship. Ahead facing us there was something that looked familiar, an alter with a tabernacle.

Visitors were allowed in the meeting place, our guide explained, speaking in English, but only the monks were permitted on the altar. The holy tabernacle, a small room, was entered only by certain monks at special times. A monk stood near our guide. He did not speak to us in either English or Japanese but with a slight nod of his hooded head seemed to agree with all she said. The grain, Mama-San Suzie clarified was donated by parishioners. Their names were displayed on the sacks to give them recognition, similar to the American church practice of listing donation amounts in a church bulletin. The grain on the floor no longer seemed out of place.

We were invited to use the time in the temple as we wished. Rather than think, my mind went blank. Standing in the center surrounded by my fellow pilgrims, I could feel the energy of the temple, a definite force present among us.

After several moments of peace in this intimate space, unaware of the others in silent prayer or tourist observations, Mama-San Suzie thanked the monk again. This time it seemed to be in Japanese. Together we moved outdoors into the sunlight. Free to walk on our own around the National Park, Mama-San Suzie in her shrill voice cautioned us with one of her many directives.

"Be extremely careful if you see any wild monkeys. They can be dangerous! Avoid any monkeys you might see!"

Monkeys-how exciting! The thought of wild monkeys did not bring me fear, but fascination. I would have loved to have met one but had little hope. Just as on the Alaskan cruise I had hoped to see a grizzly bear and saw only bear tracks, the same was expected here.

Wandering off alone, I found myself in front of a dark massive building with large double doors resembling a stable entrance. I took a closer look. The doors were closed probably locked, but I tried one anyway and it was open. Pushing it just a few cracks, I peered inside to see that it actually was a stable. The stalls were empty but I could smell fresh hay. If there was fresh hay probably a horse was nearby.

I could see in the furthest stall, the head of a white horse. My intuitive sense told me that this horse was off-limits for tourists. For fear of intruding, I closed the door.

Quickly stepping back my gaze landed above the door. I was even more surprised to see three monkeys. Not the live monkeys Mama-San Suzie warned us about, but three monkeys carved in the border above the stable door. The monkeys stood out among vibrant green, yellow and blue foliage.

The first had his hands over his ears: hear no evil, the second had his hands over his mouth: speak no evil, and the third over his eyes: see no evil. I was not unfamiliar with these little friends and neither were you. Their simple message has been communicated for centuries with reproductions of the monkeys in pictures, paper decorations or carved wooden knickknacks, similar to the one we had hanging on our kitchen door knob, the door I opened for you every day. You may remember the sound the wooden squares made when the door opened. You should.

On cue, you raised your head and licked them enough. They were a gift from an old boyfriend who frequently traveled to Japan on business and who always brought back creative presents. I never gave any thought to where The Three Wise Monkeys originated from.

Legend has it that the monkeys were cut out of a piece of wood by Hidari Jingoro, a left-handed wood carver. Perhaps the two of you have already crossed paths in the Eternal Garden above. You have so much in common such as your personal qualities. The kind of qualities friendships are built on: naturalness, sincerity, honesty, trust, admiration, sense of humor, understanding, empathy, gratitude, courage, generosity and wishing another well-- "thinking no evil."

Hidari Jingoro, just like you, lived life open-eyed, enthusiastically, and confidently. Just like you, he accepted what he had in life putting it to good use for himself and others. Just like you, he lived and enjoyed his life to the fullest. It is not surprising that he became a great artist with his artwork enduring through the ages. Legend has it that he threw himself into his work, mind and spirit, bringing to his artwork everything he had.

He did not work for money. Rather he worked for a divine Artist. He sought to express the infinite beauty of this Artist through nature: trees, leaves, animals, cats and of course monkeys.

Jingoro communicated with his hands through his sculpture rather than the spoken word making language unnecessary. The average person can understand what Jingoro is saying simply by standing in front of one of his carvings. If open and receptive enough, anyone can appreciate Jingoro's messages, deep while entertaining, and be better off for receiving them.

Hidari Jingoro was an amazing man. He still is amazing. However, if we took an opinion poll it would overwhelmingly rank him as dead and gone, in the same situation as you. In my mind, I would like to sit down with one of his pollsters and ask: "Mr. Opinion Pollster, if you declare Master Jingoro dead, no longer living, is all of him no longer living or only certain parts of him? If parts of him are buried or cremated what happened to the parts of him that were not buried? What are those parts doing now?"

In my little fantasy dialogue, the opinion pollster might look at me as if I were crazy and say, "Ridiculous. Jingoro is dead. He died hundreds of years ago. That is common knowledge. You may believe as some, that humans have a soul that left their body to go to a spiritual realm, but as far as you, I and the public regard him, he is still completely dead. No question."

The pollster might have continued to support his factual story by informing me that no one who knew the artist personally living on the mountain centuries ago could testify they had seen him alive. The pollster, if he had a copy, could present a document, a death certificate, that stated on such a date and time an appropriate authority pronounced Hidari Jingoro's physical body dead. Concluding his perfect case, he could report that the body was cremated, buried in the earth and over hundreds of years once again became part of the earth - an open and shut case.

"But what about his artwork?" I persisted. "All the inspirational sculpture and carvings his heart, mind and hands created for us humans to enjoy? Even a few non-humans enjoyed them. The art is still here with us today. On my recent visit to Nikko, I saw The Three Wise Monkeys in their full splendor. I enjoy their humor from the replica I have in my home whenever I open my kitchen door. They still convey the artist's wisdom, warmth and humor to us today just as they did hundreds of years ago when they were first displayed. I easily feel his emotional intentions in my heart. His heartfelt intentions are still a live part of him just as much as when he was walking the earth. Doesn't that say something to you according to your definition of "being alive?" In my fantasy dialogue, I get the pollster's attention while he looks at me more intently or maybe regards me as totally crazy.

"Going back to your argument that he is dead," I continued, "his body is buried. But that does not account for his spirit, the qualities that gave him his identity. Those intrinsic qualities that made him understanding, affectionate and comical, separating and elevating him to a level beyond the average mortal, were they burnt up in the blaze of his cremation? Can intrinsic qualities like that be put on a funeral pyre and then the ashes placed in an urn or lowered into a prepared hole and covered with dirt or just scattered? Those spiritual qualities are not made from that kind of material. Qualities like that are part of the infinite universe with an infinite order surrounding us continuing forever. They do not die. Would that not make Jingoro just as undying and just as lasting as his qualities? It would –wouldn't it?"

You know Mochi, if anyone stopped to think about it, the artist Jingoro is making a bigger impact on society at this writing. He is alive and making a difference, without his flesh and bones body than most of the people walking the earth today are with their own anatomy. Amazing? But not surprising when you stop to think that many humans, especially within our country's boundaries, are not able to understand that our physical senses report only a minute part of a person's substance. With our faulty equipment, we could say humans only perceive the tip of the iceberg. The true expanse, in this case, a massive abundance, goes undetected leaving us knowing nothing of our true breath, splendor, importance and value.

We are obsessed with the notion that our flesh and bones existing at birth, and during childhood, adolescence, adulthood and old age end with death. We are not coming back here. We focus on consuming. For thousands of years, our spiritual teachers have sustained that humans are made in the "image and likeness of God." To make the universe complete, this sacred image results in beings with individual identities that have eternal souls resembling the Creator.

However, amid all our shortcomings, we are making a little progress. A new interest in the afterlife seems to be emerging. We are exploring ideas based on adjusting ourselves to eternity rather than trying to make eternity adjust to us; attempting to live with the rhythm of creation similar to our more primitive ancestors. What has caused this awakening that moves us away from the belief that we are all on the right road to salvation?

Global weather pattern changes and pandemics to name a few, but one of the most far-reaching and more widely accepted reasons is from good example. The motivating behavior of kinship like you and Jingoro. Two understandable beings moved beyond borders of nationality, race, sex, age and species living lives of love providing us good examples to follow. We might even decide that yours is the path we want to go down.

I'll be seeing you...

Driving up Mt Fugi   *Photo by M. Cavallaro*

Chapter 15

GARBAGE

Fuji –Hakone-Izu National Park, Japan
Morning, October

To Mochi
Backyard in the Sky
Dear Sweetheart,

The next day of our bus tour, we traveled to

Mt Fuji. We English-Speaking humans, causing even more confusion, usually say, Mount Fujiyama. *Yama* is the Japanese word for mountain so we are literally saying Mount Fuji Mountain. Both sound foreign to Japanese who usually say *Fujisan.* You dogs never had this problem of sounding foreign since your barks have universal sound and are understood, globally.

You would have enjoyed this park because to appreciate the view of the distant volcano, we moved about in wide open space. Even though the area was immaculate you would have found delicious smells to take in. The air was clean and clear. If they used any synthetic chemicals on the grounds, their odor could not be detected.

I, like my fellow travelers, roamed along the rolling roadway overlooking a magnificent forest of what resembled short straw-colored Christmas trees. They could have been short hinoki cypresses. It is mid-October which explained the faded color. It is still early autumn and they had not yet taken on their full radiance. The brown-colored soil into which they are firmly rooted enhanced their autumnal colors. I looked further. The backdrop of dark smaller mountains leading up to the tall snow-covered peaks set against a deep blue sky, completed the unique colored panorama.

We climbed back into our bus, and made our way up the mountain to the more commercial park area from where we again disembarked. There was a long brick observation area equipped with telescopes for viewing the distant snow-capped volcano. Surprisingly there was a tourist center, which in the midst of all this naturalness seemed out of place. Out of curiosity, I quickly entered. Even more surprising was a man selling corn on the cob. Was he an apparition? To confirm he was not, I stepped up and purchased an ear.

Suddenly out of nowhere Mama-san Suzie appeared standing very close to me in a threatening stance.

"There is no garbage," she said in her high-pitched voice!

I nodded in agreement and moved outside to enjoy my corn treat. Remember how you liked to lick an ear of corn? I felt just as enthusiastic at my find as you were about the ones you came across.

It tasted surprisingly good. I munched as I walked outside enjoying the view of the solitary volcano. Although it was early autumn, it was still warm enough to wear a few layers underneath a cotton cardigan. The still thin air made this outdoor excursion a walker's dream.

From the stone steps with metal railings to the visitor buildings scattered throughout the central tourist area, everything was spotless. What did these people do with refuse? No garbage cans could be seen anywhere.

A park and city without garbage, a town without garbage, a world without garbage- seems like an impossible goal on a grand scale, but here a local reality? It seemed to me that visitors would have some refuse just as I did. No signs were posted to bring your own bag to remove your waste. What did the people do with their garbage?

After consuming the corn, I planned to take the remaining garbage, the cob and paper wrapper, on the bus where there was surely a place for disposal since most buses have waste receptacles.

Climbing back on the bus and settling into my seat, I continued to watch the panorama from my window, when suddenly Mama-san Suzie burst on me again, snatching the wrapper containing the corn cob disappearing in the back of the bus. I never saw what she did with it as the bus took off down the mountain. Maybe she carried a portable composter.

I'll be seeing you...

Chapter 16

QUIET TRANSCONTINENTAL FLIGHT

"A dog doesn't care if you're rich or poor, educated or illiterate, clever or dull. Give him your heart and he will give you his."

John Grogan, *Marley and Me*

Tokyo, Japan
Early Morning, October

To Mochi
Backyard in the Sky
Dear Sweetheart,

It was four a.m. when we boarded a small plane to transfer to Narita Airport for our flight back to the US. Too early to eat breakfast, but with Mama-San Suzie's thoroughness we found a box lunch or rather box breakfast waiting for each one of us as we boarded the plane.

It reminded me of the times I would have to

leave for a day trip early in the morning before your usual time of rising around 5:30 a.m. You were never a happy camper having to be awakened and ushered out the back door for your morning events. Just like Suzie, I would leave you your breakfast. When I returned, the stainless-steel dish which held your morning meal was always empty.

Suzie made me smile maybe because my caring for you, my home companion, was similar to her overprotective caring for us, her traveling charges.

During the short flight, my cell phone had great reception and I was able to read some troubling headlines of "Travel Bans," and "Infection Invasion." Trouble always came from the outside in. We were never responsible for any of what was going on in our country, in our hearts or our souls. Finger pointing prevailed. It was always the other guy.

Headlines at their best are attention grabbers, though often they are broadened into news-backed stories that provide valuable information, making them worthwhile. However, these stories traveled 3,000 miles to a small aircraft on an island only to provide media hype.

Sitting in the narrow but comfortable seats, I skimmed through the story finding a sentence saying our country had "gone to the dogs." There were other references to your relatives, such as "living the dog days," "dog eat dog," and "dog meat" to name a few.

This is what I was going home to. There is an old saying in newspaper writing that articles should be geared to a 5th-grade level of education. With the increased awareness and education of today's readers, the level has risen to the 11th and 12th grades.

The use of such degrading descriptions puzzles, angers, and saddens me. Those with a 5th or 12th grade level of education or even someone with no education could use kinder words. Interestingly, the value of dogs, from personal experience, observation or stories told by others, should make any human regardless of their schooling, appreciate their contribution to the quality of life.

How could a dog's unselfish love and loyalty not be recognized? Most of us humans know of these qualities. This is why we have Service Dogs, Therapy Dogs, Seeing Eye Dogs and Police Dogs, to name a few designations of superior performance and trust. Yet when we want to belittle someone, we say things like he "acts like a dog" or has "gone to the dogs."

Perhaps it would be better if we humans did "go to the dogs." We might learn something from them about how to conduct our stay on this earth. We do not have a good track record for being kind to our fellow humans. Rather we have fought war after war, even in our homeland, engaged in racism, sexism, ageism, antisemitism, and the list goes on. Our lack of compassion for one another is something you or any other dog along with me would find hard to understand. Not only do we lack compassion but we harbor violence against other members of our species. We can even be arrogant about it. Yet when we want to offend or demean someone, we say they have "gone to the dogs." Baffling!

The first mistake was to listen to or read disturbing news reports at four a.m. Many psychiatrists and psychologists have been known to advise their depressed patients, to take a break from the news, to lift their spirits.

If we wish for a better appreciation of daily life, I feel we should go farther, perhaps schedule a national speechless week, a quiet reflective in public and private week.

Everyone should remain silent, like monks in monasteries. There should be no radio, TV, theater or motion pictures. Athletes and referees in sports events could use hand signals only. Cell phones should only be used for emergency calls and computers with no audio, to write personal reflections, apologies, or caring words to others.

People on the front lines in places such as hospitals, supermarkets and the police force would speak courteously and kindly removing all the chatter. Teachers in schools should use the blackboard, computers and pictures. On a personal basis, we would communicate with our friends and family by making eye contact, using hand signals, writing notes and giving lots of hugs.

Notices would be issued from our town halls advising people to social distance or not be in the company of people other than immediate family and friends. The directive would further advise humans to spend their free time with a dog, to find companionship, fun and love. If they did not have a dog they would be advised to go to their local shelters and borrow or foster a dog for a week. They would literally "go to the dogs," in a positive sense, channeling their energy into an appreciation of the world in front of them becoming a productive member of their community and a helpful member of their family.

Stopping our endless chatter and slowing down from non-stop busy activities that make us feel important, we humans would be better equipped to perceive and appreciate day-to-day life with the warmth and meaning it has to offer rather than rushing and talking our way through it. We would also be spending more time with our dogs as I did with you. All dogs are expert leaders in the field of appreciation for morning walks, watching the sunrise, listening to the birds sing and breathing clean air.

With dogs leading us as you did, we could find our way on adventures that would eventually help us obtain a better understanding of these natural happenings, namely that they are able to communicate with us.

If we were clever enough to listen to them and follow their direction we would meet up with the Creator of our existence, seeing Him move through this world of creation surrounding us. Without our constant talking and rushing, we would hear Him speaking to us through creation just as easily as we hear the birds sing.

Could we possibly ask for anything less complicated?

I'll be seeing you...

Chapter 17

BUSINESS PARTNERS

Burlington, Vermont
Afternoon, October

To Mochi
Backyard in The Sky
Dear Sweetheart,

For a dog that is supposed to be dead and gone, buried in the earth, no more to be seen forever, you can still make quite a difference to those of us humans who are said to be alive and kicking. Today was one of those times.

My transcontinental flight set down in New York. Not ready to face my front door, I decided to take the train to Vermont, on a whim, to rendezvous with one of my Canadian cousins.

It seemed like a good idea to squeeze in a visit before returning home to New Jersey since I was traveling North to Vermont, close to the Canadian Border. I did not know at the time what an outstanding idea it was. My cousin Gabriel drove across the Canadian border to visit me in Burlington, Vermont.

As you know, I have many fun cousins, but Gabriel, affectionately called Gabby is the deadpan cousin. He lives in fear, uncomfortable in the present, and preoccupied with the past.

My father had two brothers and two sisters who were all born in Italy. He, the oldest, and his youngest brother immigrated to the US while the remaining middle brother and sisters immigrated to Canada. Gabby, the son of this middle brother, worked very hard to create a small business while living in a single-occupancy apartment in Montreal, Canada.

Gabby operated a start-up employee-owned factory that manufactured winter boots. All the employees had an equal share in the company. Some of the many hats Gabby wore included Controller and Bookkeeper. All except one of the owner-employees were cooperative. Concerning business operations that needed a majority of agreement, even though the rogue of the group was in the minority, he intimidated all the others including my cousin. His bullying stemmed not only from an overbearing personality but from his *connections* or at least the connections they believed him to have.

The outlying owner-employee was a particular problem at this time because the group, now older men, wanted to sell the company and retire while the rogue had ideas to continue business as usual.

Although Burlington, Vermont is one of my favorite cities, I would never describe it as hustling and bustling. But to avoid what he considered hubbub, Gabby suggested we meet in a quiet Italian restaurant on the lower level of a small mall.

With his dark hair, slight frame and colorful knit shirt, he exuded his usual European flare. After the big hugs and light air- kisses brushing both cheeks as was the Southern European custom, we sat in a cozy booth with the customary old-school red and white checkered tablecloth. Asking about each member of the family and there were quite a few members, brought only the most positive reports. New additions to the family, through birth, adoption, marriage, and impending marriages were the trending updates.

"How is the sale of the business going?" I

asked, waiting until the very end of his narrative, bracing myself for a different flow of energy.

"Not well, not well," he murmured. "The troublemaker will not go along with the sale."

If the majority of owners, each with equal equity wanted to sell, it still baffled me how one person could hold out and change the course of action.

"I do not understand."

"We are afraid of him," was the expected reply.

A picture flashed in my mind of a pack of basset hounds being intimidated by one of its members.

"You know if you were all dogs, you would not be having this problem," I ventured.

"If we were all what?" he asked.

"Dogs," I replied.

He looked as if he was having trouble with the language I was speaking. It was the

134

incomprehensible look of someone who not only did not know the meaning of one word but missed the whole drift of the conversation. The expression, however spontaneous could not be related to a language barrier. In addition to his native Italian, growing up in Montreal, Gabby spoke French as well as English. It was the mention of *your* relatives that was throwing him into confusion.

"You are allowing a leader to take you in a direction you don't want to go. Dogs generally choose a leader to act in the group's best interest. In addition to a leader they trust, there are usually a couple of other dogs in the pack that steer the group and 'bring up the rear' to protect the group from behind. If dogs can act as members of an intelligent team, why can't your company crew?"

At this point, I brought you into the story. Gabby's face lit up a little since he had seen your picture year after year on the Christmas cards, I sent him.

"My dog met troubling people and challenging situations all her life. She met them with her integrity, reasonableness and courage. There was never any question of what she stood for and how she lived her life. Her attitude toward life was simple. How she felt inwardly, guided her actions. Yes, and sometimes it took some courage. Yes, and every so often, there was some retaliation but she met the challenges calmly not in anger and always succeeded. Above all, she was always true to herself.

When someone came into our house," I continued, "she did not immediately go to the door and bark a greeting. She walked to my side slowly and looked up at them. Protectively, she stood her ground beside me, at all times, observed the visitor giving him or her notice of her awareness.

And as for your 'troublemaker,' do you think he will not notice your change in spirit? If he is as domineering as you say, he is probably watching your every move to make sure you are falling in line. If on the other hand, he takes you for granted, you will take him completely by surprise.

Have you and your colleagues ever considered leading a dog's life in your business endeavors?"

Gabby sat spellbound, listening attentively. He didn't say anything positive or negative. We finished our *bruschetta* and *spaghetti alla marinara*, with an espresso. Afterwards, we went

to the original Ben and Gerry's for ice cream
letting the 1960s beetle car on display open our
minds to fun memories. I then retired to my hotel
while Gabby drove back across the border to his
home in Montreal.

I'll be seeing you...

Chapter 18

LOOKING THROUGH YOU

*"You don't look different, but you have changed
I'm looking through you
You're not the same."*

John Lennon/Paul McCartney

Burlington, Vermont.
Early Morning, October

To Mochi
Backyard in the Sky
Dear Sweetheart,

     The manner in which life is lived lives after you, has been demonstrated over and over. The stuff, the strength and the impact of a well-lived, full life, are as limitless as they are deathless even if the life is "just a dog's life." You, my sweet Mochi, are once again the center of the confirmation. It happened after having dinner in that Burlington restaurant which I wrote about in my most recent letter.

I did not expect to see Gabby for a long time after his departure to Canada the previous night, but early the next morning he appeared in my hotel lobby eagerly wanting to talk as rapidly as possible. Expecting the border to close at any moment because of the unstable public health situation, he wanted to talk quickly. What did he want to talk about? He wanted to hear about *You* and your inner character.

Maybe mentioning your character strength just as he and his colleagues needed some fortitude was perfect timing. Perhaps he had been searching for a long time and you provided an answer he liked. Whatever the reason, there he was at my hotel again, after braving the hour's drive from Montreal to Burlington, more frantic than usual.

What caught his interest the night before was my description of your success as a popular neighborhood figure related to what was going on inside of you rather than what was happening on the outside of you. Your completeness of character rather than your exterior observable physical features enabled you to calmly enjoy our house, backyard and neighborhood.

This may seem like a trivial circumstance: a dog enjoying her backyard and neighborhood. We did not live in a bad area but rather in a picturesque community with a hint of 1950s tranquility. You also did not go into an office every day, work on a factory floor or wait on demanding restaurant customers.

Although Gabby knew of your contentedness and your "getting alongness" solely from me, he was always impressed by the success of your exploits. You never ran away or tried to escape from your home to find freedom, you were happy with where you were. A wagging tail and smiling face greeted friends and family entering our house while a tail pointed upward and eyes opened wide to receive service people. On our neighborhood walks there was no pulling back on your leash when people or dogs approached nor was there any hiding behind bushes or any showing of teeth with territorial behavior when visitors, animals or people entered our back yard. Mochi, somehow a light went on in his brain to help him understand and connect how your inner qualities brought about this gentle conduct.

As we sat at a little outdoor café near my hotel Gabby suggested I write down all your character strengths while he itemized the character traits of his company employees. My job was easy. My list was endless with the merits of your character easily coming to mind. I'll mention a few to give you the gist of my work: simplicity…freshness... big-heartedness… honesty...genuineness…freedom from restraint…decency…determination… focus…not giving up.

After we sipped some coffee, we discussed the striking un-doglike attributes and differences, his co-owner employees possessed apart from, 'the trouble maker'. Gabby scribbled almost in an obsessive state, a list of negative and unsavory attributes. He held nothing back about his colleague's worst behavior and most cowardly manner. His list was so raw and distasteful that I chose not to print it since it added nothing for the reader.

Gabby sipped more coffee as he mulled over the two lists, mentally picturing his colleagues. Suddenly he pushed his cup away and slowly leaned back with a resigned but amazed expression in his eyes and stature.

"I have been writing about myself," he said, surprised. Perhaps writing it all down brought it home or, perhaps, the unthreatening comparison to a dog was the charm.

Speechless, there was nothing I could think of to say. It was not surprising, since I had suspected that all along. The group was not able to stand up to the agitator because their leader, my cousin, was thinking fearful thoughts and acting on them like a weakling, not showing any leadership. Before I could overcome my bewilderment, he stood picked up the check and took out some dollar bills.

"I have to take charge," he said. "I have to return to Montreal immediately, but I'll be in touch. Please excuse me." With that he turned and quickly disappeared, walking out of the hotel café.

What enabled him to recognize his own behavior, I later learned, was yours. If you, a dog and committee of one so to speak, could be honest and true to yourself, while bringing security, happiness and comfort to those around you, namely me why couldn't he? True, you had no pack of your own to lead unless you considered me your pack. However, you certainly made an impression on almost everyone you met. Standing low to the ground never made you appear to be less powerful but rather sturdier. Your sweet face and agreeable look were usually met with similar looks in return. True you did not deal with seedy potentially violent characters on a day-to-day basis, but you certainly calmed down and won over the strangers and neighbors you met.

Gabby called a meeting in the usual conference room, to unite the owner-employees, minus the agitator and closed the door. Since the group did not know you, Gabby used the example of what even a dog could bring out with the most right inner and outer matching qualities, conducting one of the most unique business meetings in the history of entrepreneurship.

Later he told me the meeting was one of the most life-altering experiences that he had ever gone through. Rather than everyone being defensive, each man opened up to this examination of conscience. They got in touch with their inner thoughts and feelings as honestly as they could; not an easy job for a group of men. Not only were they willing to share their findings, but they seemed to enjoy it.

The consensus was that they were so fixed on the behavior of the agitator, placing all the blame on him, and never giving any thought to what was going on in their own minds. Their thought processes they considered separate never taking into account that their thoughts, whether professional or personal were part of their being.

Thoughts determine observable outward behavior such as body language or tone of voice.

This group had been conducting business in their mental underwear totally unaware. They had given very little, if any, thought to the reality that they, like all of us, could see as well as be seen in a see-through world. They gave very little credence to the understanding that the bodies and minds we spend so much time exercising, dieting, beautifying, and obsessing about exist behind a thin veil. Anyone even minimally shrewd not to mention someone as experienced as the agitator, could easily look through and see what is going on inside and take full advantage of what they see.

Even with this enlightenment, they told my cousin they still believed they would have difficulty standing up to the errant partner. Mental strength was somewhat new to them, but they were willing to try.

At this point, Gabby admitted that he too might have a little difficulty, but if they stood together, proud, resolute, calm and united, he felt their energy would not only reach the errant partner but the universe beyond them. They could manufacture their success just as they were creating their defeat. My cousin is very articulate when he wants to be.

Gabby called the partner in question and informed him, not in his usual quick nervous voice but rather with a calm firm tone, that the rest of the owners wanted to meet again to discuss the sale of the property. Even before they entered the conference room, the partners cleared their minds of any negative thoughts and filled them with single-minded good energy. One by one they entered the room, each with a confident body carriage. The last partner stood in the rear waiting till his co-workers were seated then decisively closed the door and sat in the last remaining chair. With his experienced perception, it took very little time for the offending partner to realize his bullying days were over.

The company went up for sale that day. Even with impending economic difficulty, the economy does what it wants to do and not only one buyer but several buyers appeared. Once again, the attitude and behavior of "only a dog" paid off.

I'll be seeing you...

Chapter 19

WINDOW SEAT

Vermont/ Canadian Border
Mid-Morning, October

To Mochi
Backyard in the Sky
Dear Sweetheart,

I'm chugging along from Northern Vermont to Central New Jersey, settling into my seat on The Vermonter train. Out of the rail car window, I could see the greatest and the greenest views of the Green Mountain State--waterfalls, narrow roads bikers love, and rural towns.

As a child, whenever traveling on a train with my brother, we always played a "window game" whereby we made up stories about the cars or trucks we would see. We pretended the cars or trucks were ours and we were driving them to exciting places such as a candy store, the supermarket or the post office. I drove the car while my brother drove the truck.

Traveling by train was not the way you came into my life. How you arrived from Minnesota, as confirmed by your papers to where I met you in Red Bank, NJ, I always guessed was by car or van. It was no grand entry by any means. Many puppies like you traveling from a broken-down puppy mill such as where you started from, with little or no immunity risk picking up a disease along the way, never reaching their destination. You arrived with kennel cough and ear mites. Whether you started the journey sick or caught a highly contagious respiratory disease on the trip, I would never know. The owner of the pet shop had you treated by a local veterinarian which probably saved your life. She wouldn't have made any money with a dead dog.

Many times, returning from visits with my relatives in Montreal, Canada, I traveled by train. Even though I did not cross the border on this trip home I felt the old strange feeling, that a new world lay beyond. With shaded light entering the windows, the rhythmic movement of the rail car made a specific destination goal meaningless. It was easy to reminisce. For a few fleeting minutes, as the train slowed approaching the border, I looked out of the car window at the green leaves on the large mature trees. The shadow of the leaves added to the feeling of being in the wilds: The

dividing line seemed vague. Feelings of being in
neither country brought uncertainty, freedom and
change; the feeling of belonging nowhere.

The train stopped. Silence filled the car only
to be disrupted by the sudden loud opening of the
car door. Enter the border patrol. Men and women
dressed in dark military-like uniforms walked up
and down the aisle: Intimidating.
Where are you going is the standard border patrol
question. Both the Americans and Canadians ask
it.

"To my home in Princeton, NJ," I answered
when asked. My unspoken response was, "Going
home to my dog."

So many times, I took this trip from
Montreal to Princeton coming home to you. I
arrived at midnight and took a taxi, which pulled
into the driveway of my house. I carried my bag
up the front steps. Despite the late hour, when I
opened the door there you stood. You looked up at
me sleepily wagging your tail. After receiving
several hugs, content, you turned slowly, walked to
your bed and went back to sleep. On this trip, that
ritual would not take place.

I settled further into my seat on the

Vermonter and rolled forward. The fleeting feeling of being in no-mans-land dissolved my thoughts of entering an empty house. Instead, my memory shifted to your undaunted puppy playfulness on your first day home. Even sick you bumped around with your short legs, floppy ears and long body. Somehow you got them all coordinated to run wildly in my backyard as soon as we arrived in Princeton!

Forgetting to play can have long-term negative effects on people as well as animals. Life with you never allowed that problem to present itself. With your backyard and in-house antics, you made it easy to laugh every day.

The couple seated across from me could have certainly used your comic abilities. They bickered with each other ever since we left Burlington. Nothing pleased them. They found fault with each other as well as the inside and outside of the train. They certainly could have used a visit from one of your relatives to distract them from themselves and open their eyes to the beautiful immediate world around them. I think I know what their problem was. They had been among *their* relatives too long.

This condition is quite common among the

human species. They infect one another by their preoccupation with status, perception of happiness or success on their terms, and what life should be. Many people like this would turn to stress relief activities such as yoga, meditation or counseling, to name a few, when in reality what would benefit them most is some dog therapy. Under canine care they would be able to see and move about their day with a smile on their face, seeing their world for what it is and being grateful for it.

The scenic name of this train seems to be wasted on these passengers. It surprised me to look down the aisle and see very few people taking advantage of the natural beauty. One woman was knitting, a couple were playing cards, and one young man with eyes closed, had his earbuds plugged in while another man with no visible listening device appeared to be in a trance. The rest of the passengers were asleep. Only two were looking out the window enjoying the heartwarming Vermont scenery and one of them was reaching for her newspaper. The windows may well have been covered with cardboard.

Mochi, I always wondered what you saw when you stared out into space intently looking at something. Your gaze was not like the vacant look in that fellow passenger's eyes. You were absorbed by whatever your focus was on. Your body as well as our eyes were part of the gaze while you sat so still with your head tilted to the side, slightly raised. You could have been in another world and you probably were. If the highest accomplishment of vision is to see God in everything, you may have been much more accomplished than I ever imagined.

Whenever we traveled in the car, you always looked out the window with amazement and excitement. The train windows were wasted on the humans. Dogs like you would never let those windows go to waste.

Your puppy playfulness, I believe was what helped you heal from your kennel cough and ear mites, not to mention your sprained cruciate ligament, your skin allergies, your ear infections, your arthritis, glaucoma and loss of hearing. The twinkle in your eyes never left. If silliness and playfulness helped you, they might have been worth a try on the *people* seated across from me.

I'll be seeing you...

Chapter 20

TRAVEL'S END

Right now, I'm in a different place
And though we seem far apart
I'm closer than I ever was...
I'm there inside your heart

E.E. Cummings

Princeton, New Jersey
Early Morning, October

To Mochi
Backyard in the Sky
Dear Sweetheart,

    This letter marks the end of my travels. About an hour ago, at midnight, an UBER brought me and my bags from the train station to our little cape cod. The ritual of carrying suitcases up the front steps into the house officially marked the end of my Cross Country and East meets West global travel. From here on everything that happens in the future will be part of another episode.

Right now, after a few hours of sleep, I am sitting at the kitchen table in the early morning sipping tea. My bags are in the spare bedroom resting until I get the energy to open them later today. It will be easier to go through the contents of my suitcases and do laundry than it will be for me to arrange the thoughts and memories of my journey and completely understand them.

Collapsed at the wooden table in a morning stupor, I'm wondering if my travels were real or just an incredible dream. Maybe that is because I visited so many different places, one after another, doing so many unique things. During my travels, I encountered so many contrasting reactions mingling with people from various regional backgrounds and cultural beliefs while peaceably exchanging our differences.

But what fascinated me the most was being able to interact just as closely and learn from the collection of animals both domestic and wild, I encountered, dogs, cats, horses, deer, raccoons, snakes, living creatures which my fellow humans call inferior life forms.

This letter, especially the closing part of the paragraph, would probably require some explanation if it were written to one of my kind. It might even generate some unflattering name calling directed at me, such as eccentric or less diplomatically, "out of her mind." On the other hand, writing to one of your family members would be understood. It would also be appreciated, I feel certain, by the freer thinking individuals of my species who can think higher than their low-hanging mainstream rooves and further than the boxed-in mental limits of the masses.

It always mystifies me that some of my fellow humans, especially from my own country, who have unlimited educational and travel opportunities can be so unaware of or unconcerned about life forms that are different from their own. With all our progress we have not made many inroads into the rewarding relationships we can have with the nature that surrounds us. The birds in our backyards can very well be 'chirping in the wind'.

There may be many varied reasons for this based on how our country developed, but the bottom line of the issue may be based on our feelings of entitlement-everything was made for us. Everyone and everything in the environment, birds, cats, dogs, cows, fish, earth, trees, oceans and skies were made for our needs while everyone else's needs are secondary. Lofty claims block the ability to see how lacking in intelligence some individuals are, those who fail to appreciate the extent of intelligence possessed by creation that is non-human.

Most humans with exposure to some religion, if they slow down enough to think about it, believe in a vague way that a universal force of some kind is responsible for creation, all creation. The Supreme Being that gave life, energy and balance to humans, gave the same life, energy and balance to the rest of creation.

Yet some humans feel that the Almighty and powerful Entity uses only the human species for communications and motivation for actions. They separate themselves assuming they are a form of life higher than the oceans, the skies, the atmosphere, the earth and all those that inhabit them. Quite an arrangement! What would members of the non-human species have to say about that?

Free and forward-thinking humans do not share this opinion. They believe that the Supreme Being's power is everywhere at all times and in all places. Not only do they listen to their own species but they open their hearts and minds to the language of the Eternal Creator who they believe speaks to them through all of creation whether it be human, animal, environmental, dog, cow, ocean or sky.

Some of us believe that the original Garden of Eden was a place of this kind where communication came naturally. Very few words needed to be understood and to understand. Thoughts were read and feelings were felt making words unnecessary. Of course, the world was a lot simpler than it is today with our global environment. But even today, aren't humans still human and have the same need for peace, love and harmony? To confuse things further, even in the simplistic Garden of Eden something went very wrong, thus we were destined to arrive where we are today, far from Paradise.

The original Garden of Eden was in such disarray that it needed to be re-invented. Let me repeat a familiar excerpt from one of my human species' favorite books, the Bible.

Genesis 6:13 And God said to Noah, "The end of all creatures of the flesh is on my mind: the earth is full of violence because of them. I will destroy them with the earth."

6:14 "Make an ark of resin-wood; make it

tight with fibre and cover it with pitch inside and out; ......19. Of every sort of living creature of all flesh, you shall bring two into the ark, to keep them alive with you; they shall be male and female. 20. Of birds according to their kind, of cattle according to their kind, of every kind of creature moving over the ground, two of each will enter with you to be kept alive."

Note here that Noah did not go out and call the animals like Tarzan summoning his apes nor did he go out and trap them. The animals just came. Their Creator directly communicated with them.

How do we recreate paradise right here on earth? Putting to use some of the things I learned from you, Mochi when traveling around the country, as well as outside its boundaries, brought me the solution: I filled my mind with good thoughts! Whenever people, animals, trees, wind, or rain crossed my path I tried to mentally connect with them as they approached, pouring out complimentary thoughts.

Moving about with this invisible yet powerful mentality gave me a sort of internal unseen, letter of transit, a mystical visa that afforded me safe travels. From the time I entered the departing flight door of the airport, to opening the front door of our house a little while ago, I did not meet up with any unfriendly members of my species or yours. Whenever I moved about with good intentions, spoke from my heart and offered reasonableness, I received back in kind even from other than two-legged animals.

I could go on forever telling you about all this, but the day is passing, the laundry needs to be done and here comes my neighbor with her dog who will be demanding his treats. This will be the last letter for a while. I had a wonderful time with the sunrise, canyons, wild horse range, canal paths, volcanic mountains, glaciers and all the rest of nature, and hope nature enjoyed having me as part of it. If it did, it is because of everything I learned from you about how to see love in creation beyond my own kind. I am forever grateful to you, my sweet Mochi, for being you.

I'll be seeing you...

Acknowledgments

I wish to thank the people and animals who made this book possible:

Danielle Wood whose excitement to read the finished product spurred me on to finish the book as well as to publish it.

Honey, Danielle's horse, who was a huge consolation immediately after Mochi went to another world as well as offering comfort long after.

Nancy Genovese, editor;

Julia Poulos who encouraged me to keep writing my personal journal which was the foundation of this book. The journal is named "Happy Thanksgiving," started on the first Thanksgiving without Mochi.

My beta reader, Diana Rosenberg for her insightful reactions.

Lisa Weston whose computer skills helped prepare the book for publishing.

A sincere thank you to those who reside in another place but remain in my heart and mind:

John R. Long, the sender of daily emails of encouragement often with links discussing book authorship and publishing.

Robert E. Thorpe who only said kind things about my entrepreneurial efforts throughout our friendship of over 30 years.

Finally, I want to thank, *Mochi,* my strong heart, who guided our relationship with endless inspiration. I love you forever.

Photo by Frank Sauer

Mary Ann has been a nurse for over a quarter of a century with a second career as a computer consultant. When she transitioned into the retirement phase of her life , she wanted to actively pursue her life-long love of writing. After several years of freelancing for newspapers and magazines, she decided to focus on publishing her first book, *What My Dog Told Me About Healthy Eating,* the story of how her beloved basset, Mochi, helped change her eating choices.

When her long-time sweet companion crossed over

the rainbow bridge, the author felt it only natural to create another volume as a tribute and exploration of pet death. Mary Ann hopes by sharing her stories of appreciation and travel adventures she will help others feel better in their sadness.

As an animal lover and advocate for healthy eating she founded her church Vegetarian Ministry, in the town where she lives, Princeton, NJ.

Bibliography and Resources

J. Allen Boone
Letters to Strongheart 1939
Kinship with All Life 1954

Wallace Sife, Ph.D.
The Loss of a Pet fourth edition 2014

Elisabeth Kubler-Ross
On Death and Dying 1969

The Holy Bible
Genesis to Ruth, Job to Sirach and the Prophets
Translated from the Original Languages with
Critical Use of All the Ancient Sources by
Members of the Catholic Biblical Association of
America
Fourth Edition 1961

Information on Pet Loss

Association for Pet Loss and Bereavement
https://www.aplb.org

Information on Basset Hounds

The American Kennel Club breed information
http://akc.org/dog-breeds/basset-hound/

Tri State Basset Hound Rescue
http://Tristatebassets.org

Suggested Reading

Mary C. Neal, M.D, *To Heaven and Back*

Joe Dwyer, *God, Shebly and Me*

DISCUSSION QUESTIONS

-Did you enjoy the book? If so, what impressed you. If not why?

-Where you immediately drawn into the stories or did it take a while to get into them?

-Have you recently lost a pet?

-Did the book bring out any emotional responses?

-What main themes does the book explore?

-Did the narrative help you explore any of your philosophical beliefs?

-Did the book take you outside of your comfort zone?

-What feelings and beliefs of the author did the Grand Canyon confirm?

-How did Honey provide healing?

-Did any of the human characters in the story remind you of anyone you know?

Discussion Questions

-Did the meeting of Mochi and the deer remind you of any confrontation you have had?

-What places have you visited that felt spiritual? Why did they feel spiritual?

-Did the role Social Media played in the unfolding of events seem natural to you or did it surprise you?

-Did the book inspire you to visit any of the places mentioned such as The Grand Canyon, Glacier Bay, or Nikko?

-Are national parks important?

-Do you feel people live on through their artistic creations or other works?

-The Japanese tour guide was vigilant not to leave waste behind. How do you feel about composting and protecting your immediate as well as greater environment?

-What was the strategy the businessmen used to neutralize the partner who bullied them? Did the reaction of the bully surprise you?

-Do you think playfulness is important in

relationships or our outlook on life?

-Does seeing the good in someone or something help you to view them or it more objectively?

-What do you think the future holds for the author in view of her relationship with Mochi? Do you think she should get another dog?

-If you read reviews before reading the book, did you agree with the reviews or not?

-If you were going to halve the size of your book collection, would this book stay or go?

-If the order of the travel were reversed with the journey beginning in Vermont and ending in the Grand Canyon, would the impact of the events be any different?

-If you could ask the author a question, what would you ask?